THE FIRE STILL BURNS

A LIFE OF TRAIL TALK AND CONTRARY OPINIONS

Chilco Choate

Heritage
House

National Library of Canada cataloguing in publication data

Choate, Chilco, 1935-
  The fire still burns

    ISBN 1-894384-07-5

    1. Choate, Chilco, 1935-   2. Chilcotin River Region
(B.C.)—Biography. 3. Outdoor life—British Columbia—Chilcotin River
Region. I. Title.
FC3845.C445Z49 2001   971.1'7504'092   C2001-910048-5
F1089.C42C56 2001

First edition 2001

Heritage House acknowledges the financial support of the Government
of Canada through the Book Publishing Industry Development Program
(BPIDP) for our publishing activities. Heritage House also acknowledges
the support of the British Columbia Arts Council.

Cover and book design by Darlene Nickull
Edited by Chuck Hart

Heritage House Publishing Company Ltd.
Unit #108 – 17655 66 A Ave., Surrey, B.C. V3S 2A7

Printed in Canada

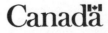

DEDICATION

For the Ranchers of British Columbia

Considering that we have so far survived our "interesting times" together with our lives, it seems only fitting to thank you for making my life as interesting as it has been, and I do hope that I helped to make yours the same. And a toast to whatever bluebunch wheatgrass and grizzly bears have managed to survive too.

It takes a big woodpile to winter in the Chilcotin bush. The building shown here is the cookhouse at Choate's Place. It is equipped with a wood cookstove, a wood heater, and, recently, a propane cookstove as a backup to the other.

CONTENTS

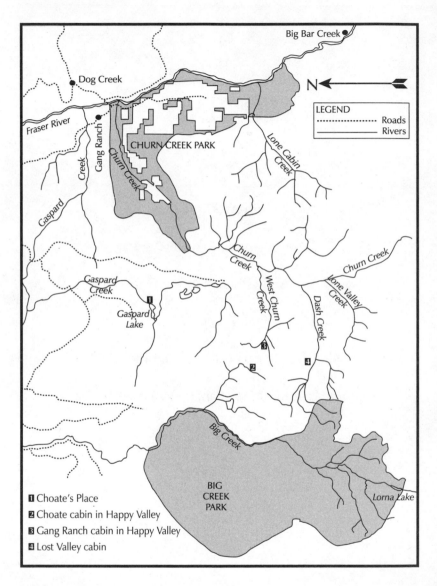

Chilco country.

FOREWORD

Chilco Choate, The Man

My first taste of Chilco Choate was over two decades ago, riding through the pine and spruce forests of the Chilcotin Plateau on very rough tracks. Travelling on horseback across the magnificent highland landscape west of the Fraser River was a perfect contrast to my urban life as a commercial airline pilot. We were in the Gaspard Lake area when I first ran across big yellow discs nailed high up on trees with the word "CHOATE" painted in red or black. These puzzling discs were the tops of 45-gallon drums, coated with yellow paint. I rode the country for another year before discovering through word-of-mouth that Choate referred to a person, not an animal, and that Chilco Choate was a reclusive hunting guide, living smack dab in the middle of the Gang Ranch territory, reputedly the largest cattle ranch in North America.

I decided to seek out this Chilco Choate creature. Next year, I rode back up north and stopped to ask a salty-looking fellow in an old pickup if he knew where I could find Choate's place. He replied that he was Choate and, after a short measuring session, he invited me to his camp. Thus began a relationship that I came to treasure more each year. Choate is a remarkable man, with a propensity to take on politicians, ranchers, logging companies, and all who would threaten his precious Chilcotin. His six-foot-plus frame, booming voice, and sharp mind are enough to intimidate both bureaucrats and corporate executives.

About the time I met him, his hearing had begun to fail after a life of gunfire and unmuffled engines. Eventually, he had to abandon one of his favourite areas of confrontation, the "Land Use" meetings; he could no longer hear the speakers.

I suppose the real measure of a man is how he handles himself under stress, and it was under such conditions that I learned to respect the grit inside this campfire storyteller. Years down the trail from our first meeting I found myself invited on one of the last big rides that Choate hosted after his retirement from the hunting and guiding business. The party consisted of myself, Choate, my wife, my eight-year-old daughter, two other women, Choate's dog, and twelve horses, half of them used for packing our food and gear for the week-long trip. Choate led off each day, his hearing aid turned up so high that we could hear high-pitched feedback as he rode ahead, unaware of his sonic beacon. Our route toured the Gang Ranch wilderness in the southern Chilcotin Mountains. The measure of the man showed in his responses to all the wrecks that accompany such a trip. One time, our panicky pack horses got stuck in a mud hole, then burst free, charging through scrub pines, scattering packs, canned goods, and yellow-painted camp gear. (Choate covers everything he owns with yellow paint.) Another time, as we camped deep in the mountains, the horses decided to head home, so they popped their picket pins and thundered off into the twilight. Choate, always gentle, polite, and tireless, kept his cool and the whole menagerie together. And rest assured: when the campfire burned, he spun a yarn or two.

I'm still struck by his love for all life, and for the living of it. I give you, Chilco Choate.

—Peter Marshall

THE LEGEND OF OLD NERO

S teve Johnson was mounted on one of his favourite horses and riding a long way out in front of the boss, which had become the customary place for him to be. I should say this was his favourite horse when there was nothing critical to do: the mare was strictly a show-off piece, a nag that loved to prance along with her head high and her tail cocked up like she was heading for the Williams Lake Stampede. There wasn't a brain in her head. She was virtually useless as a hunting or trail mount, and in our world that pretty well spelled out the probable content of her life to come. Steve broke this mare and, once he'd begun to identify her numerous faults, named her the Bay Bitch, which turned out to be a most appropriate name.

A hundred yards behind, the boss was plodding along on his old reliable, at that time a big bay gelding named John Henry. As was also customary, for reasons now long forgotten, it was the boss's job to drag along the two pack horses carrying our camping and trail gear. Whoever was relegated to that job automatically became the "tail-end-Charlie." It was a well-known fact that Steve Johnson hated leading a pack horse, and the thought had often surfaced in my mind that maybe it was no accident he almost always rode a horse that was unsuited to leading others. In fact, that may have had a lot to do with how he came to be the "guide leading the guide" most of the time. Well, what the hell! He was good at it. So without comment from either of us, that had pretty much become our permanent relationship.

This was the year that I had become a self-employed businessman, which meant that I had elevated myself up, or thought I had, from being someone else's hired hand. I was the new owner, which was supposed to translate into meaning the BOSS, of a hunting and trail-ride guiding operation that I had been working for over the past three years. The previous name of the outfit was the Gang Outfitter. It had never been part of the Gang Ranch, but the "Gang" part of the name was certainly meant to imply that it might be, or, more realistically, to position its operation area on the map. The first thing I did when I became the boss was to drop that title and use my own name instead. That many not have been the wisest decision, but I was only 23 years old and not the brightest person in the country. As time went on I discovered that there were many other things in this world that I was ignorant of. This Gang Ranch that I refer to, if you do not already know, is one of Canada's larger ranches, but by no means the largest as various owners of it would like the world to think. Geographically it begins west of the Fraser River, 65 miles west of Clinton, B.C., and it holds a grazing licence that covers about a million acres of Crown land.

Steve Johnson, who is often referred to in these stories, was a friend and work partner when the former owners held the camp, and he was still now supposed to be relegated to the position of the "hired hand," but that was a title that often became blurry over the next several years. There was never any doubt in my mind, or in the minds of my parents who lived in Clinton, that given the opportunity, Steve Johnson could easily have run an operation of his own. He was not the only assistant guide of this new operation—there were other short-term assistants—but I will concede that Steve was my top or head guide when I wasn't around. After his death twelve years later, his position was taken over by a friend of both of us, Jimmy Seymour of Canoe Creek. Jimmy worked for me for over 30 years.

On this particular ride-out, during the early fall of 1958, we were in the Gang Ranch area of the Chilcotin and heading up into the high country to do some game scouting. This was the best excuse we could come up with to go there, and when the Chilcotin weather breaks clear in late summer and early fall it's an easy excuse to fall back on. The previous day we had sniffed the air, tossed powder into the wind, and come to the unanimous decision that the time was exactly right to go do it all again. We weren't wrong about that either. First day out and there we were riding down the centre of Hungry Valley, soaking up the glorious scenery and revelling in the feelings of contentment brought on by such days—the kind a person wants to last forever. You drift along in such a wonderfully mellow mood that you can slip your mind to wherever in the universe you want it to go. I've personally experienced thousands of days like that, days we've come to refer to as Indian summer.

Travelling along in this dream-like state, I was jolted back to earth when John Henry came to an abrupt stop in a muddy creek. In the middle of the crossing, the hired hand and his fancy horse were blocking the trail, with Steve turned halfway back so he could face me. There was a big grin on his face when he asked, "Do we need a tag for a Sasquatch?" I don't recall the facial expression I was trying to portray, but before I could answer, Steve nodded down toward a track in the mud. "Holy Christ!" I thought. Something with snowshoe-sized feet had recently walked down that creek.

We moved our horses up out of the crossing and both of us bailed off so we could examine the tracks more closely. We knew they weren't from Sasquatch, but the size of the imprints was impressive all the same. The tracks were still distinct and created the overwhelming feeling that we'd stumbled onto the trail of what must have been the biggest grizzly in the country. Because they were so much larger than any tracks we'd ever seen, we marked their length and width on an axe handle to be sure there would be no after-fudging of the figures. We cut small notches into the wood so the exact measurements could be verified later with a tape.

We'd remounted and were moving up the trail again when Steve laughed back at me and said, "Think you can handle

This is not a photo of Old Nero—as far as I know, no human ever shot him with gun or camera—but it is a good likeness of what huge grizzlies look like. A hunting guide's rule of thumb to estimating any bear's age is first to determine if the belly hangs low or high. If it appears to be high or concave, then it's probably a young or famished bear. If the belly hangs low, as it does in this photo, then it's an older bear. Another pointer is to try and estimate if its head appears large or small against its body. If the head appears to be big, then it's probably a young bear; if it appears to be small, it will be an old or very big bear. Bears' heads and feet seem to grow faster than other parts of their bodies.

that one with your .30-30?" He could afford to laugh—he was riding a faster horse and packing a bigger rifle, which happened to be a .30-06. He wasn't dragging a couple of reluctant pack horses along behind him either. But I simply grinned back and replied, "Whoever gets him breaks the record book," and we nodded in agreement.

After that we rode along in silence for a while, our minds returning to their respective realms. Mine went back to memories of conversations with Gus Piltz, who still owned the Sky Ranch over near Big Creek. The first time I met Piltz, three years earlier, he'd mentioned something about a huge grizzly, one that had taken to visiting the Sky Ranch calving grounds almost every spring in the previous few years. These veal forays proved sufficiently costly that Gus had apparently been offering a $500 reward to anyone who could bring the marauder to justice. I heard a couple of other fellows in the area, Jim Russell and Jim Bishop, mention something about this offer, but so far nobody had been able to cash in on the reward.

Because of the way Gus described his unwelcome visitor, especially its size and cleverness in avoiding its just desserts, I'd taken the whole story with at least a few grains of salt. But now, having seen those tracks, the implications were enough to make me wonder. Pretty soon there wasn't the slightest doubt in my mind that such an enormous bear really did exist, and this realization made me begin to reconsider some of Gus's other stories as well, tales that, at the time, I had perhaps not taken seriously enough. A person has to be careful about things like that.

Putting aside Piltz's problems and offer for a moment, it seemed to me there might be a way to exploit this new situation and turn it into a figure somewhat larger than $500—even though most people would have considered that to be a great deal of money in 1958. It was to me, especially since I'd only that year gone into the outfitting business. As a consequence of that decision my finances were strung out on such a thin, tight shoestring that the twang often woke me up at night. That $500 was sure tempting, but the allure was tempered by the knowledge that turning those tracks into quick cash was by no means a sure bet.

And so it was that with a slightly devious mental turn I began seeing those tracks leading not so much toward a bear, but toward something more like the goose that lays the golden eggs. Do you believe in killing that kind of goose? Well I don't either. So I shifted my thinking into higher gear and more than likely added quite a few years to this goose-bear's life.

By the end of the day's ride, which had brought us up to our cabin in Lost Valley (or Dash Creek as it's named on the maps), a plan had pretty well jelled in my mind. It was simply this: to leave the bear as he was in the hope that he would continue living within my allotted guiding area and keep making lots of those platform-sized tracks along the trails. Being a hunter myself, and realizing what the sight of those pad prints had done to both Steve and me, it wasn't hard to imagine how they would stir up our hunting dudes. Perhaps the tracks by themselves could be turned into trails of gold or, more literally, the continuous cash flow my banker kept harping on about and that I clearly did not yet have.

At that time I was charging $500 for a two-week hunting trip. The way the seasons were laid out, there was room for two trips in the spring and two in the fall. Because of sheepherders' poison and ranchers like Gus, however, there really weren't enough grizzlies left to warrant such liberal seasons. This was especially so if every hunter expected to be successful. With things as they stood it seemed the government was, in actuality, selling sportsmen hunting opportunity rather than high success rates. And if that's legal for the government, then why not for others, too?

Viewed from this perspective, it only required lots of those huge tracks and ongoing luck on the bear's part and there could be a bonanza for both of us. So that's the way it was decided. See how easy it is to ride up a sunny Chilcotin trail and become rich as you are doing it? It can be rainbows and pots all the way!

Later on that evening, secure in our Lost Valley cabin, we measured the marks on the axe handle and recorded the bear's paw size. The length of the hind foot was seventeen inches, and both the front and the back feet were eleven inches across. The largest tracks we had ever recorded prior to that were fourteen inches by eight inches. This platter-foot specimen—so long as its body size related to its feet—was going to be a great deal bigger than any bear we had ever seen before. In all probability it would make it into the record book, assuming, that is, that some hunter was lucky enough to kill it.

With all these factors fresh in mind, I decided it was time to run my business plan by somebody else to see how it might take. Steve being the only other person in the valley, it didn't take much to figure out whose ears should receive the first pitch. I saw my opening and laid it on him as he was chewing on a steak bone and gazing out the window. When I was done he didn't say anything for a few moments, and it was obvious he was mulling the idea over in his own mind. Finally, though, he nodded in agreement. "That's a pretty good plan," he said. "And anyway, any bear that has lived as long as this one has, and eaten as many Gang Ranch cattle as it has, deserves to be allowed to die of old age." (Since Steve had done a stint or two as a Gang Ranch cowboy, he and I shared several like-minded opinions about the value of cattle in wilderness areas, not to mention our further lack of appreciation for the ranch owners and their new manager.)

Thus far in agreement, I then began relating some of the stories that Piltz had told me about what I assumed was the same bear. From the stories we'd heard, and the figures we had to play around with, we tried to figure out how old that bear might be. In the end we decided it must be somewhere around 30 years old, which we knew was getting on for a wild bear. That night, as we lay in our bunks being entertained by the overly friendly mosquitoes, we were still hyped up and talking about this bear, a prize grizzly that was at that moment somewhere close by. Steve told me a story he had recently read about a similar-sized bear, one that had led ranchers and bounty hunters on a merry chase through the U.S. cattle country for years before someone finally killed it. That American bear had been given a

Results of a hunt at Lost Valley camp. The griz was not Nero, but the biggest we ever took, with a skull measure of 25.5 inches. The deer at the left had our largest antler width, at 35 inches. The lucky hunter was J.D. Fisher of Texas. At the right is Jimmy Seymour, my assistant and a long-time friend.

name (which I have now forgotten), and winding up the story, Steve suggested we lay a name on this one, too, as it might make the sales promotion easier to pitch. Well that made good sense to me. So we lay there for a while and lobbed different names back and forth. We debated names like Bigfoot, Squatch, Beefeater, and even Old Gussy (in honour of Gus Piltz), any one of which would have been appropriate. In the back of my mind, though, there was an epic story of a Roman rebel, and I kept trying to remember his name. This Roman had been a renegade slave, had escaped to the mountains, and from there had turned on his masters and made Rome tremble. This bear being an obvious rebel, it seemed to me that the story was a good fit and that the Roman's name might serve well.

That night the only name I could dredge up from memory was Nero, even though something kept haunting me, telling me he was not the right Roman. When I suggested the name and history to Steve, he didn't take to it at all. His rationale stemmed from the high probability that *a)* this bear had never been to Rome and *b)* nobody over there would even know what a grizzly was. So why try to draw them falsely together? But I'd made up my mind and, being the boss of our outfit, I pulled rank.

The following morning some Gang Ranch cowboys dropped in to visit, and in the course of conversation I tested the entire bear story on them, complete with its new name. These fellows were a good bunch of cowboys and saw the entire plan for what it was: a good lark for Choate to lay on "those rich Yankee hunters." At the same time, they warned us that if they saw the bear first, they intended to collect Gus Piltz's bounty. As of that moment, Old Nero of the Gang Ranch/Big Creek country became formally recognized and named into our vocabulary.

About a month later I tried the story and pitch on one of my best client-friends, "a rich Yankee hunter" who went by the name of Bill Norton, from Seattle. Bill began to laugh as he informed me, "Aw hell! The Roman you're trying to remember is Hannibal." And of course, he was right. For a while after that we tried renaming our gold pot to the more appropriate name, but it was too late. By then the story was spreading all by itself, so the huge bear remained sort of misnamed.

As it turned out, my plan was a good one, at least from our perspective, because it eventually became every bit as lucrative as we'd imagined. I do not recall exactly how many hunters came and paid their dues for a sporting chance at trying to collect that world-record golden hide. Over the next several years there were well in excess of 30, but as fate would have it, luck was always on the side of the bear and the outfitter. There were even those odd occasions when we made a little more effort towards actually bagging the bruin. Since several of our clients had become good friends, we naturally had qualms, like: "Should a person do this to a friend whose booze you are then partaking in?" But such thoughts we usually rationalized away by convincing ourselves that the hunters were getting a sporting chance at meeting Nero. At least sort of ... Well, think about it this way. Considering we were all out there in the same bush, there was always the possibility that the bear might just walk out in front of us, even walk into camp. Things like that. And that would have landed the rainbow straight into the hunter's pot.

In the end, though, we were able to sell a lot of sizzle and keep the steak, and Piltz's bounty turned out to be a paltry sum compared to the way we conducted matters. In 1958, for instance, I was charging $500 for a Nero hunt. A few years later, after inflation began setting in, the price went up to US$3000. Hell, it got to the point that I even used to consider Nero part of the family, a rich uncle who was sharing the wealth and that sort of thing. Would you cash in your rich uncle before it was necessary? So there you are!

A Legend in the Making

Over the ensuing fourteen years, Nero's reputation grew with every cow that died or was killed in the high country. The Gang Ranch cowboys gave him full credit for most of the deaths, even though over in our camp it was common knowledge that there were other marauding bears doing some of the killing. And we knew that far more cattle died from ingesting poisonous weeds than from bear attacks. Beyond that, bog holes and outright quicksand take a high toll, too. In those days, though, cowboys refused to acknowledge such losses. When bears got the credit the cowboys were encouraged to go bear hunting, which is a lot more exciting than packing salt, fixing fences, and other such chores. Sometimes they hunted for bounty, too, because the Gang had gotten into the act as well.

The first person from our camp who set eyes on Nero was one of my assistant guides and a long-time friend, Jimmy Seymour. He was guiding a pair of moose hunters up in Lost Valley at the time. The year would have been 1961 or '62. I was hunting out of the same camp, and my hunter was the one who had come looking for bear (you can guess which one). This hunter's name was Dan. One afternoon, about halfway through Dan's hunt, we decided to take the rest of the day off. Although we'd seen lots of nice tracks, we had not sighted a single grizzly, much less Nero, and Dan was growing weary from hunting what he was beginning to describe as "phantom bears."

We rode into the yard and the first thing that caught my attention was that Jimmy had his entire horse string all tied up and saddled. It looked as if he was getting ready to pack up and pull out, even though there was still a week left on this hunting trip. There was no sign that his hunters had bagged their moose either, so the situation appeared strange at first glance. It gave me an odd feeling, knowing there'd been no previous plans to split up the party.

After tying up our own horses, Dan and I walked over to the cabin, opened the door, and, looking inside, saw Jimmy and his two hunters finishing their lunch. I noted their three bedrolls were all rolled up and ready for packing—proof they were preparing to leave. Jimmy never said a word and barely moved, other than sticking his head deeper into his soup bowl. But those two moose hunters jumped right up and proceeded to give me a tongue-lashing. Let me tell you, those two guys were steaming mad. According to their account, "This Indian guide you left us with goddamn near got all of us wiped out by the biggest grizzly in the world." They did not seem to be the least bit impressed by the fact that they'd become a couple of God's chosen few just to have met such a bear and been allowed to survive the encounter. Even after I tried to reason out a few like-minded suggestions for them, their hype was not dampened one little bit. The old standby—assuring them that "if you don't bother a griz, the griz won't bother you"—didn't work either, as one of the moosers retorted back, "Like hell they won't! Down in the States those goddamn things kill several people in Glacier and Yellowstone parks every year!"

By this time Dan could no longer contain himself and jumped into the conversation on my side. "Yeah," he said, "but up here it's a different situation because you guys have a pair of .300 magnums that will make sure things like that don't happen to you. Why hell, man, you guys missed an opportunity to collect what might be the world's record grizzly." That didn't help matters much, though. One of the moosers now turned on Dan,

Lorna Lake (top left and right) is the liquid jewel of Big Creek Provincial Park, which ranchers said would never exist. Big Creek is one of B.C.'s newest parks and one that I proposed, expanding the oldest undecided park proposal in B.C. Whoever makes it to Lorna Lake has arrived about as close to heaven on earth as they are ever going to get. This lake, and the area around it, is still as wild as it ever could have been. Graveyard Valley (lower left) in Big Creek Park is one of the most beautiful alpine valleys in the country. This photo was taken in mid-July of a cold 1990s summer

when the snow line in Graveyard Valley hardly receded and grass remained about nil—hardly enough for marmots to survive on. Just the same, Gang Ranch cattle are licensed to go there and take what they can. The lower right photo shows the view from Dash Plateau, looking over the upper end of Big Creek Park. At one of the last public "Land Use Meetings" that I attended in the Big Creek community hall, one of the ranchers addressing the meeting screamed, "Nobody wants a park in this area except that goddamn Choate."

laying a finger up against his chest and replying, "Look you big fuckin' fool, my brother and I aren't up here on some kind of power trip like some other people are. All we came here for was to bag a truckload of meat, so we're getting the hell out of this valley. As far as we're concerned, you and Chilco can stay right here and you're both welcome to our share of every fuckin' bear in the country."

The mooser then turned to me and said in a calmer voice, "So right now, Chilco, you are going to explain to Jimmy where he can take us so we are not going to be meeting up with one of those goddamn things again." He turned back to Dan and began appealing to us in a more rational way. "Why that goddamn bear we saw is big enough to peel the door off this cabin with one swipe of its paw."

If he was trying to scare Dan down to his own level it didn't work, because Dan's reply to that was, "Well I sure as hell hope he comes and does it because my ass is getting saddle sore from riding around looking for him." The quip was lost on the moosers. One of them started getting fired up all over again and he challenged Dan and me with a kind of hypothetical-wish comeback. "Well I hope you stupid bastards walk right into that thing on the path to the shithouse tonight!"

The conversation went round and round that way, with nobody giving ground, until I knew for sure there was no way those two moosers could be talked into reconsidering their plans to move out of the valley. We agreed the next best thing was to have Jimmy pack them down into a lower valley, either Hungry Valley or our base camp at Gaspard Lake. Jimmy opted to go all the way to Gaspard, and I suspected that choice was because my wife, Carol, was there, and she would then be doing the cooking and camp chores for them. Jimmy hated cooking for other people.

I suggested they stay in Hungry Valley—there was a better chance of bagging a bullmoose because of the lesser hunting pressure. Both moosers had been quietly listening to Jimmy and me discussing these options, and one of them now butted in, asking whether there was any chance of bumping into a grizzly

The Hungry Valley cabin, which was part of the old outfit that I bought in 1958. It was built by Sam Grypuik in 1948 and burned the year after I sold the business.

down in Hungry Valley. "They never cross the mountain range between here and there," I assured him. At that point, Jimmy, being the loyal hand he was, ducked his head deeper into his soup bowl to hide the grin on his face. One of the moosers turned to his brother and, nodding in obvious satisfaction, reset the tone of the discussion by stating, "Okay then, Hungry Valley it is. We'll meet up down there with whatever is left of these guys at the end of the week." And that was what we all agreed to do.

When we had finished our lunch and the conversation had cooled to more civil levels, Jimmy and the two moosers treated Dan and me to the story of how they had come upon the grizzly. It went something like this.

Early that morning they had been riding up a small brushy creek, looking for bullmoose, when Jimmy, being in the lead, stopped his horse and began focusing his binoculars on something farther up the valley. He quickly dismounted, tied his horse to a tree, and while doing so, silently signalled the others to do the same. The hunters at this point assumed they were about to begin stalking a moose that was somewhere up ahead. Jimmy was not carrying a rifle, but he did have a 28-inch axe that all our guides carry in a scabbard on their saddle. When the hunters saw him withdraw it, they did likewise with their rifles, chambered a round, and set their safety catches. Not a word was spoken. Jimmy stepped right into the creek and motioned the hunters to do the same. Very cautiously, he proceeded to lead his crew up the creek. Every once in a while he would stop, motion the hunters to stay low, and sneak another peek through the binocs at whatever it was they were stalking. Apparently he never did offer the hunters the opportunity to look for themselves, and they never pressed the issue, instead letting Jimmy make all the decisions.

They had waded up the creek a fair distance before one mooser's curiosity began to overpower his caution, and since he had never seen a bullmoose, he decided he wanted to get a look at one before the shooting started. So at Jimmy's next reorienting peek through the binocs, this mooser decided to take a peek too. Because his feet were now freezing in the water filling his boots, he was thinking of taking a longer-range shot to get out of that creek as soon as he possibly could. When he saw Jimmy slide back down into the creek and go into a sneaky sort of crawl, he figured that between his freezing feet and the power of his .300 magnum, they had to be close enough to the moose to get him. And anyway, his brother was there as backup.

So the mooser stuck his head up to take a look, and what he saw was clearly not what he had come all the way up here to collect. Right up ahead, less than 100 yards away, was a huge dark-coloured creature feeding on a dead cow that was lodged in the creek. At that moment the enormous thing must have sensed something was amiss, because it reared up on its hind legs and came eyeball to eyeball with the hunter. Rather than the horn spread he was hoping for, the mooser saw a large piece of rotten flesh hanging out of a gaping mouth that contained rows of remarkably big teeth. "Oh, God! For a split second I felt like I was going to sit down in the creek and shit my pants," the hunter admitted. "Why, that goddamn thing was standing twelve feet tall and looking straight down on us. Not only that, it was only about four big jumps away, too."

Fighting the compelling urge to sink backwards into the creek, he managed to reach out, touch his brother, and, using sign language, quickly make him understand what was about to happen. Jimmy was by now too far ahead to signal, and the mooser said he was afraid if they called out to him the bear might attack. So as silently as they had gone up the creek, they turned and retreated back down it. "If the goddamn guide wanted to see a bear killed, he could damn well tackle it himself," he said. "After all, he still had that fuckin' axe."

Jimmy told me his version of events later, when we were alone. "I was guidin' my hunters up to this really big grizzly bear, and I figured to get them real close so they can't miss it. We was doin' really good, too, because when I got up to about 50 yards, I figures it's close enough. So I turns around to signal them hunters to start shootin,' but I ain't got no hunters. I see those bastards is all the way back to the horses and gettin' ready to leave me there with nothin' but my axe.

"So I stuck my head up to look again, and I see the bear is watching them hunters and not me, so maybe the bear don't know I'm there. So I sits down behind a bush and waits. When them hunters get onto their horses and start to leave for camp, the bear, he grabs a big piece of cowhide and takes off the other way. So I went back to my horse and come back to camp too, because my feet is damn near froze." Jimmy shook his head in disbelief and lamented, "All that goddamn work for nothin.' Goddamn chickenshit hunters!"

That being the story, I had to quiz him further about the bear. "Jimmy," I said, "everybody talks about how big this huge bear is, but how big is he, really?" As I asked, I stretched my arms out, inviting Jimmy to demonstrate just how high and long the bear might be. Jimmy thought for a moment, then sort of shook his head and replied, "Oh, he's big all right. Big as a bull!" I knew he was referring to the domestic Angus bulls the Gang Ranch were at that time ranging in the area, and at first it seemed a ridiculous comparison. On the other hand, I'd read about grizzlies shot in earlier days that had topped the 1,800-pound mark, which would certainly put them in the same weight range as domestic bulls. In my mind, I compared bears we had taken on other hunts, whose paws measured eight inches wide, with the eleven-inch width of this one. After considering all the angles, it was easy to conclude that we had a *very* big bear for a neighbour.

But that was it for that hunting trip. The two moosers and Jimmy moved down into Hungry Valley, where they were able to bag a bullmoose without being challenged by Nero or any other bears. Dan and I stayed up in Lost Valley and watched over the dead cow for another week, but the only bear that came near it was a black bear. Dan shot it instead, and dreamed of Nero for another year.

Grandstand View

I didn't actually see Nero myself until the following summer, when I returned to Lost Valley alone to cut the season's firewood and tighten up the pasture fence before the cattle arrived. This would have been about mid-June, and I was working on the woodpile when a small herd of cattle came walking past the cabin, heading down into the lower part of the valley. Their arrival was early as there was not much feed for them, and yet it was not that uncommon because Gang Ranch cattle control was still almost non-existent.

Once the cattle were turned out of the winter feed yards onto the open grassland, the stronger and wilder ones usually began roaming in an upward direction, following the higher edge of the green grass line in the same way migratory wild ungulates do.

This might also have had something to do with the wilder and smarter cows wanting to keep their new calves far away from the cowboys' branding irons and cutting knives for as long as they possibly could. By fall, cows don't seem as protective of their calves as they do when they are younger; perhaps they figure it's time for their kids to begin fending for themselves. That's pure speculation on my part, of course, as it's debatable how smart cows are. I do know for sure that only a few are natural leaders, the rest are followers. (So are cows like us, or are we like cows?)

The scene at Hungry Valley camp during one of those cold fall hunting trips into Hungry Valley in the 1960s. It was below –40 and we bagged 5 moose within three days of hunting. It was so cold that we could ride only about five miles from camp before we had to stop, build a big fire to warm up, then ride back to camp. The moose must have been cold too, as they just stood in the meadows and let the hunters blow them away. We do not get weather like that anymore.

Anyway, this small herd of cows arrived ahead of the main herd, choosing to compete with their natural enemies rather than the two-legged ones that were following along two weeks behind them. Since all of this had happened many times before, there was no reason for me to be particularly surprised to see these early arrivals, but I always took note of when, where, and sometimes why these things happened the way they did. In this case there were about twenty cattle, some of them with small calves following, which made them wary of me. All the same, they drifted right on by, clearly heading down into the lower end of the valley.

Cattle at Gaspard Lake. They are considered to be "range locusts" when too many are left in wild country for too long.

I forgot about them till about an hour later, when the same herd came stampeding back up the hill, charged past me, and headed up the trail towards Hungry Valley. Some of the cows were sweated up, too, with their tongues hanging out. This was a strange sight, enough so that it raised my curiosity to the point where I stopped working and began backtracking, trying to discover what their problem might be. I was fully expecting to discover that a bear or wolf attack had started the stampede; there seemed to be nothing else that could make cattle behave that way. I collected the only gun in camp—a .22 rifle we used for clearing packrats out of the cabins—slung my binocs around my neck, called my big collie, Kim, and set off down the hill.

Cattle running over soft ground through the timber made easy tracking for about a mile. There the trail reached the edge of the open valley of Dash Creek, and I walked out onto a high, open ridge. It was a perfect lookout over the valley, and directly below was a pair of huge grizzlies feeding on a recently killed adult cow. The distance between us was only about 150 yards, but Kim and I had the advantage of height, wind, and noise from the creek, as well as cover from the timber.

We immediately ducked under a thick, bushy pine tree that had branches right down to the ground. It took only a moment or two to convince Kim that he did not have to chase the bears away to protect me, and he dug himself a cozy nest in the squirrel shavings piled up under the tree and curled up in them. Making myself comfortable in the shavings alongside, I loaded a few more cartridges into the magazine of the .22, just in case. A .22 is almost useless in a bear attack unless the barrel is actually shoved down the animal's throat and fired, but it can serve as a noisemaker. I know from personal experience that if a bear is inclined to be turned away by noise, there is nothing better than a gunshot to do the job. I would rather have a .22 than an axe or a club, that's for sure. An even bigger gun is better by far, but you have to make do with what's available. On this occasion, rather than a bigger gun, I wished I'd had a camera. Without one, eyes and memory were left to do all the recording.

Luckily for Kim and me, the two grizzlies were totally engrossed, tearing the cow carcass into smaller pieces. They seemed to be in a race with each other for what they must have considered the choicest pieces of the dead animal's guts, because those were the parts they devoured first. Closer examination made me realize that describing these bears simply as "huge" was an understatement, especially when you think of normal bears. The larger of the two was a dark brown colour, almost black, and it likely would have appeared black from a greater distance, with only a tinge of frosty silver on its neck and shoulders. He was obviously male, or a boar as they are sometimes called. The other griz was about three-quarters the size, a beautiful, mottled, brown-to-brown sow. She showed much more silver than the boar, displaying the typical grizzly frosting over her face, neck, and all down her back—as beautiful a blond as I have ever seen, but perhaps not one to meet on a dark trail.

The claws on both bears were long enough to be seen without aid of binoculars. From the size and colouring of the boar, I thought he might well have been a drifter from the coastal inlets. Bella Coola, Bute Inlet, and Knight Inlet, where the world's largest grizzlies have been recorded, are only about 80 miles west of that part of the Chilcotin. Wildlife biologists have told me that grizzlies from those areas are almost colour-coded for identification. That said, from my first sighting of those two bears below me that day, I knew instantly that I had finally met Old Nero.

That was the first time in my life that I'd had such a grandstand view of grizzlies behaving as they naturally do, and all in broad daylight! So woodpile be damned: Kim and I just hunkered down for the day because I knew there might never be another one like it. It did not take the bears long to get the cow well laid out, and like dogs do with a fresh kill, they frequently rolled all through the sloppiest parts of the innards. They were enjoying themselves in all the blood and guts. They played around with their food the way small children do and showed no aggression toward each other at all.

They were having so much fun that I even began thinking thoughts like: "What a nice thing it would be if Kim and I were to go down there and join them." But I quickly realized that it might not be such a wise thing to try, and we stayed put. Just the same, the sight and the feelings emanating from the bears were contagious. Up to that time I never would have suspected that bears are such social creatures, but they sure as hell are. For me, this was a kind of "continuing education" course that was worth whatever it cost, because the way they fed and played was only part of what they taught me.

These two bears were also mating. When a person watches something like that it's only natural to compare it with your own feelings under similar circumstances. I was able to watch them go through the love up to the full sex act, which was an eye-opener. It surprised me that grizzlies enjoy the ritual just as much as we do, and do it all pretty much the same way, too. Having witnessed other animals going through the sexual act, I'd learned that for most wildlife it's fast, sometimes violent, and makes you wonder why they even bother with it. But these bears soaked into it for twenty minutes to half an hour at a time, and even then it wasn't over. Then they sat back on their haunches, wrapped their forelegs around each other, and proceeded to lick all that gucky, gutty, gooey stuff off each other's faces and necks. Not all that different from what you or I might do in the shade of a cherry tree on a nice summer day.

Those bears displayed other human characteristics as well, showing off and trying to impress each other with demonstrations of strength. The cow they had killed was about four years old and must have weighed more than 1,000 pounds before they opened it up and drained most of the juices. Yet several times Nero took a good mouth hold into the centre of its back and proceeded to lift the entire carcass clear off the ground. He would give it a good shaking, throwing more blood and guts all over both of them. Every time he did this, Blondie was so impressed she would bounce right over and lick all the goo off Nero's face, neck, and ears, and her appreciation was such that it usually started the two of them into that other ritual again.

Once, when Blondie was trying to tear a front leg and shoulder off the carcass and it would not come apart for her, she just sat there in what looked like a pleading pout. Soon enough, Nero walked over and took hold of the opposite leg and they proceeded to have a tug-of-war until one of the shoulders did tear loose. That made a strange sound. Even at 150 yards or so it was loud enough to wake Kim up, and he acted like he wanted to head down there and help them out. Luckily I was able to grab him and quietly persuade him to go back to sleep.

Then there must have been a change in the wind or something, because both bears suddenly stopped feeding and reared up onto their hind legs to sniff the breeze. They didn't seem to detect anything alarming, but that moment gave me a true estimate of how high a big bear stands and, by God, let me tell you again, it is impressive. Looking through a pair of seven-power binoculars at 150 yards on a clear day left me in little doubt that Old Nero stood well over ten feet to the top of his head. By stretching his neck and pushing his nose up in the air, there was no question that he could reach another two feet higher. Old Nero sure was a lot of bear.

It still seems hard to believe, but by the end of that day there was so little of the cow left that Nero and Blondie were satisfied enough to simply wander off in separate directions, leaving the scraps to a flock of ravens that had been gathering. She went down the valley and he headed up, and from my last sight of Nero I swear he had a swagger. He was projecting such an air of complete confidence that I could only assume what he wanted next was either a good fight or another female.

The following day I went back to inspect the site for any further information that might be gleaned from the experience. All that was left of the cow was a large piece of hide that had been licked clean, along with the skull, backbone, leg, and shoulder bones. Most of the ribs had been snapped off and eaten, likely by coyotes that packed them off during the night. Other than that, the only evidence of what had taken place was the large piles of "bear sign." From the size of them, it seemed both those bears must have had bungholes the size of stovepipes.

So that was my introduction to Old Nero, and I've never felt disappointed by it.

Horse Bait

Over the next few years, a steady procession of hunters who wanted to put their names into the record book were lured here by those huge tracks or by the stories they heard about them. And there were the Gang Ranch cowboys to take into account— they would have shot Old Nero on sight at any time of year. Considering that several other people I know had also seen Nero at one time or another, I eventually came to the conclusion that he was more lucky than smart. On several occasions even I could have shot him legally.

A number of moose hunters came within range under almost the same conditions as the hot-tempered brothers I've already told you about, but every time Nero left himself exposed, it seemed always to be for the benefit of moosers who weren't interested. Whenever we had a hunter who wanted nothing more than to nail that bear's hide to the wall, Nero seemed to become nocturnal, because his tracks simply disappeared. Maybe he was telepathic or something. Whatever it was, he got the message and left the area for a while.

Sometimes he was gone for long periods, but that didn't surprise us. Wildlife biologists, using radio tracking collars, have confirmed that boar grizzlies often establish a circular range that can be as much as 200 to 300 miles long, and they might only pass through a given part of it once or twice a year. This is especially true in the dry Interior country, where natural bear food tends to be scarce. Grizzlies are continually on the prowl for a feed, a fight, and in midsummer, for satisfaction of that other basic urge. If you and I will admit to the honest truth for a moment, it all comes down to realizing just how similar their lives are to ours.

Some later experiences will give you a better idea of just how smart (or lucky) this old bear was, and you can judge for yourself. Like I said, there were times when we did make a serious effort to help our hunters tag Old Nero. Bob and Rocky, client-friends from Portland, Oregon, came on at least four occasions to try their luck. On one of their later hunts we knew from his tracks in mud that we'd lured Nero to a horse we'd killed for bait (at that time it was legal). Even with the bait laid out in a perfect location, though, things were still not going as we'd hoped. It was turning out to be another of those times when Nero was acting "oh so clever!"

On this occasion he decided to become a midnight snacker. We arrived at the bait site every morning before daylight, and returned in the evening to keep watch until full darkness, but Nero eluded us every time. As a matter of fact, we never even caught a glimpse of him, although there was plenty of evidence that he'd been there: our bait was rapidly disappearing from one location and reappearing in another in the form of huge piles of bear sign. After his third successful feeding, we knew we had to come up with a better plan or this hunt was going to end up like all the previous ones. Another of those "chalk up one for Nero, zero for the hunter" deals again. Since Bob had been on three other "zero" bear hunts with me in the past, he was beginning to get cheesed off. The impending probability that this one was going to turn out the same way had both him and Rocky getting vocal on the subject.

Late evenings in the cabin they would lean on me a bit to, perhaps, bend a few rules and laws so the odds might turn in our favour. Their major proposal centred around Bob's big, six-cell flashlight, and they had a couple of good, rational arguments why we should use it. One was that if one of my paying clients (such as Bob, for instance) did not collect Nero's hide soon, then one of the Gang Ranch cowboys was bound to luck out ahead of us and collect the ranch bounty that was still on offer. We all knew from direct conversation with the cowboys that they had no qualms about bending any rule in the book. They were all packing guns, but hardly any of them bothered buying a licence, much less a bear tag. Paperwork and game wardens were mostly a big joke in the cow camps. All of this was hard to dispute.

The other argument, a kind of thinly veiled threat, was the suggestion that continuing to take influential hunters out on zero hunts could do damage to an outfitter's reputation. Furthermore, Bob would reason when I was finally ready to accept the light of economic reality, what other hunter could I think of who was more entitled to this bear than he was? The way they had it figured, they already had about US$20,000 invested in Nero, so it was about time Choate mended his ways and dropped the charade of being so goddamn prudish. After all, everybody knows laws and rules have always been made to control other people, they'd reason, and if they aren't bent once in a while, game wardens, cops, and lawyers would soon be out of their jobs. They might even have to find real, honest work for a change!

You might think such lines of thought are put forward in jest, but when you have one of your best client-friends with his hand on your shoulder and the other keeping your glass filled with nothing but the best, it becomes mighty easy to finally see the pure, white light of reality. So my decision was made.

The next afternoon we made up a stack of sandwiches for supper and the following day's breakfast, then rode up to the meadow where what was left of the bait still lay. We also took along our sleeping bags as it was mid-fall and the night temperature at an elevation of 6,000 feet can be nippy. We picketed the horses about a half mile away on a lower meadow, then walked up to a good ambush site. There we got well positioned and bedded down for the coming vigil, which we referred to as the "bear watch." The hunters each had a rifle, while I had the six-cell light, my skinning knife, and a hunting axe. With something just over a smidgen of luck, before the week was over Nero would be relocating 600 miles south, down to Portland, Oregon.

Peering out in silence, all three of us stayed awake until well after midnight, but there was no sign of movement across the meadow. If anything approached, especially an animal as big as a bear, there was enough natural starlight to see it. The intense watching was beginning to tire our eyes, however, so we decided to take our turns at the bear watch, allowing the other two to catnap. We settled on two-hour shifts, mine being the last, which would take us through to daylight. I soon dozed off, leaving the other two to keep tabs on what might be going on across the meadow. It was agreed that under no circumstances was anybody to use the flashlight until we knew for certain that it was time to do so. A misfire would surely spook a bear like Nero, and in all likelihood he would never return again.

When I awoke later on in the night I discovered both hunters snoring logs off. Perhaps that was what woke me up. Bob was a big-bellied man and could really do justice to that type of job. Soon we were all sort of half-awake, and we could hear the horses down at their end of the meadow snorting and whistling. We could tell from the sound that they were alarmed, and that woke us up in a hurry. As I got the six-cell positioned, I could hear the other two checking the safety catches on their rifles. There we lay, tense and at the ready for about an hour, but with no sign of movement across the meadow I eventually drifted off to sleep again. At 5 a.m., a hand shook me awake to announce the beginning of my official watch. The others assured me that during my snooze nothing had moved across the meadow. I lay there expectantly: I was sure this was the time of day when the action was most likely to begin. But as my watch ticked on and nothing appeared, it was beginning to look like we would be repeating the whole procedure again the following night. Oh well, that's the way it goes, I thought, consoling myself with the notion that if success comes too easily it's not really appreciated. This could all be viewed as whetting the appetite.

With the greying of daylight, which at that time of year happens about 6:30 a.m., visibility comes slowly. By straining my eyeballs through Bob's 7X50 mm, Bausch & Lomb, night-and-day binoculars (at that time the best money could buy), I could see that things across the meadow did not appear the way I remembered them from the previous evening. When I cautiously stood up in my sleeping bag to get a better view, I learned for sure that they had changed for the worse. I awoke the other two and they jumped up with rifles at the ready, but the silent shake of my head told them that wasn't necessary. A sighting through their rifle scopes confirmed what I already knew—that somehow, some way, we were already too late. It was now light enough to sidle over to where the bait was, but the evidence there only confirmed what we already suspected: we had no bait to watch over. Apparently that goddamn bear had snuck in sometime during the night and dragged the remainder of the horse carcass about 200 yards back into the thick timber. He then proceeded to clean the last meal off those bones at his leisure, and the game was up.

I had no doubt that the hunters' snoring was to blame for spooking the bear, and I told them so with no mincing of words. But Bob was not about to buy that theory. The way he had it figured, our failure had more to do with the sleepy-headed guide, and he emphasized this in a number of ways, such as informing the guide that he was beginning to wonder what the hell he was paying the guide for anyway! As we were saddling our horses and preparing to head back to the shack, he gave me his parting shot. "This is the fourth horse that I've paid a hundred dollars for to feed your goddamn bears and coyotes and it's the last one I'm buying, too. If I ever come back here to try for this smart son of a bitch again, then we'll just feed him a couple more Gang Ranch cows."

Another bear hunt season ended, and Nero was once more scratching his marking tree with symbols that meant "Another horse, another year."

The following year I laid out a horse for a different hunter in exactly the same place, but this time I was smarter about it. It was another one of those years and hunts when I was leaning in favour of the hunter. Perhaps it was time somebody collected this trophy, or at least got a shot at him, I thought. I bought a bigger horse this time and laid it farther out into the meadow where it would be clear of the early morning and late evening shadow from the trees. After only a few days, tracks and signs appeared and it was clear that the first bear to the bait was none other than Nero himself. The trip was rapidly shaping up to be a memorable hunt.

Unless you come across it by accident, a bear's first feeding on bait should be granted as a freebie. It seems that bears need that first feed to take possession of bait. After that, many become so possessive they will not run off at all, although not all bears react that way. Whether it's intelligence or just plain hunger that makes the difference, we still do not know. In any event, we never began any bear watch until the quarry had that first free meal.

We'd gathered this bait intelligence over the years by observing other bears that were neither as lucky nor as intelligent as Nero, because we had stretched out a few lesser grizzlies. Some of them happened purely by accident, some through planned baiting that worked like a textbook case, and a few by hair's breadth luck on our part. When I say hair's breadth, I'm referring to instances where the bear seemed as wily as Old Nero, but in the end it was still the hunter's luck that took the field. When our efforts focused entirely on Nero, we always felt that we were dealing with The Old Man of the Mountains. That being the case, he was always the teacher and we were the students.

On this occasion we didn't expect him to return to the bait the next night: bears seldom do. Usually they'll take a huge feed off a carcass and then wander off for a few days, returning to feed at intervals until the carcass is finished. This time, though, Nero did return the following night for a second nocturnal feeding. And once again he dragged what was left of the carcass back to his favourite dining spot in the thick timber. By the time we located it, there was still at least 1,200 pounds of carcass left, and it was all Steve and I could do to get our saddle horses to drag that carcass back out into the meadow. Considering that Nero had taken possession of this carcass, we took our chances handling it. We drove a wooden stake three or four feet into the ground and tied the dead horse's back feet to it with a halter shank. With that much human scent around, we were sure that a bear as wise as Nero would this time take a few days before returning to feed. He certainly would not reappear out of pure hunger, because he had already eaten and spread out about 500 to 600 pounds of horsemeat and guts.

The following morning we all went moose hunting, planning to check the bait each afternoon when we returned on horseback from our moose excursions. That turned out to be another poor decision. The first afternoon, even as I rode up, I could see that— lo and behold—there was no bait! It was not hard to discover why. The Mountain Man had simply pulled the stake out of the ground and dragged horse and stake together back to exactly the same dining spot as the day before. By this time the carcass had been whittled down to about 1,000 pounds, and the only good thing about that was it made it easier to drag it back to the meadow again. By now we, too, were getting smarter, and this time we tied the bait to a good-sized tree. We began the bear watch in earnest, but as the hunter hadn't pressured me into using the six-cell system that year, we reverted back to rising earlier, going to bed later, and not sleeping on the meadow with the bait.

The honest truth of it is that I have never, to this day, killed an animal by pit lamp, and I don't relish the idea at all, especially when you're dealing with an animal of grizzly bear calibre. Aside from the possible legal consequences, my attitude stems more from the safety aspect. In the dark, even using a light, it is not easy to make a sure and deadly first shot, and it is unlikely there will be a decent chance of a well-placed second shot. Since the behaviour of a wounded grizzly is well recorded, it doesn't take much to imagine the danger of that situation when you throw in a hyped-up hunter—one who is probably nowhere near as experienced or brave as he implied before the shooting started.

It could all too easily wind up in an erratic case of buck fever, with disastrous consequences for both hunter and guide. (I'll have a few things to say about that subject later on.)

Suffice to say, I still much prefer any type of daylight hunting to a shady midnight affair. And, of course, with the illegality of six-cell hunting, trouble is never far away. Even back in the deep bush, a hunter would do well to consider the value of his wallet and, maybe, his freedom before being so tempted. There's always a big risk when there's a witness. My philosophy is that when two people (and read that as *any* two people) know a secret, then there *is* no secret. Shifty things seem to have devious ways and reasons for somehow leaking out.

So there we were, trying our best, and yet the tied-to-the-tree system didn't work either. Three nights later Nero returned to the bait, and this time he simply chewed off the rope and once again dragged the carcass back to his preferred feeding area. By now we didn't even have to follow the drag marks, but rode straight to where we knew the carcass was going to be. Given that both time and bait were running out on us, we were becoming a little concerned. The bait, in particular, was a worry as it was now down to about 800 pounds. On the upside, it only took one saddle horse to drag it back to the same tree, and this time we tied it there with heavy fencing wire.

But that didn't seem to be the answer either. It was as if he were always watching us from some vantage point. Two mornings later, when daylight arrived, the two hind legs were all that was still wired to the tree, and there was only enough meat left attached to them for raven pickings. Again, we rode directly to where we knew the rest of the carcass was going to be, only this time there was an astounding surprise awaiting us. That huge bear let us come crashing up to within 50 yards of him—and there were two other large grizzlies with him.

The three of us saw Nero plain as day—he was standing in a reared-up position—but the other two were more nervous and waited only long enough to take a good look at us. Then they took to their heels. Nero acted almost as if he were going to challenge us, but when his buddies left he slowly dropped down on all fours and followed them. That was a lucky thing for us, because we were in thick timber and our horses were spooked. If one of the bears had charged, we would have been in serious trouble. By the time we'd dismounted and drawn our rifles from their scabbards, the bears were long gone. It made for a few exiting moments—coming upon three huge bears at a 50-yard distance does give your heart a flutter or two. Especially when it's all over and you know that events could have ended with drastic consequences.

After we'd calmed down and taken stock of our circumstances, we discovered that the carcass was all but completely cleaned up. It had been torn into several pieces and scattered all over the bush area, so there wasn't enough left to serve as bait anymore. It appeared to be all over for another Nero hunt. This time, though, the hunter did at least get a good look at him—almost eyeball to eyeball—and that was enough to bring him back to try another year. Unsuccessfully, of course. That's the way "fair chase" hunts go sometimes, but it's not all so bad, because the outfitter and guides get paid just the same, and that's what it's all about, isn't it?

Stumps and Totems

Jimmy Seymour had a different sort of amusing go-round with Nero when he was once again guiding a mooser. We were all hunting out of the same cabin in Hungry Valley at the time. Since the cabin is located right in the centre of the 25-mile-long valley, when there is more than one guide we divide the territory: one of us hunts to the east and the other to the west, or north. This time Jimmy had a single hunter and it was his turn to go east, so I went west, both of us hunting only for moose. I received most of this story from the hunter himself, a dentist from Seattle, but Jimmy was sitting there listening to the hunter's rendition and he never disputed a word of it.

According to the dentist's version of events, they rode down the valley about four miles to where there is a large brushy meadow that runs right up into the mountain. The Lost Valley trail follows the edge of this meadow for quite a distance. When Jimmy arrived there he decided to hunt on foot since parts of the meadow are too brushy and noisy for hunting on horseback. So he stopped and tied the horses to some trees. The idea was to circle the meadow and return to the horses, a route that would take a couple of hours. The mooser loaded his rifle, Jimmy grabbed his axe, and off they went.

It was early morning and there were still a few patches of fog and mist swirling over parts of the meadow as they drifted along, examining each section as they came to it. There are areas where you can see quite far across the meadow, but in other places the willow brush is high and dense—places where a hunter can easily miss seeing an animal, even one as big as a moose. Since a moose can suddenly appear out of nowhere, you have to hunt slowly and cautiously.

Jimmy had his binoculars and was scanning the meadow methodically, but he was having no luck locating a moose. The mooser, meanwhile, was relying on the naked eye, which at those distances in poor light makes for poor hunting ability. Yet as the mooser studied one of the larger meadows, he noted a low mound over on the far side. It was covered with some windfalls that had a large, dark-coloured stump in the centre. He couldn't see the stump too clearly at first, but the mist was now lifting. As visibility improved, each time he saw the stump anew he was surprised (and laughed to himself) at how much that stump resembled his daughter's big teddy bear. And wasn't it amazing that although his viewpoint kept changing as they moved along, every time he took another look from a fresh angle that teddy bear stump always seemed to be looking directly at them?

The mooser found all this to be very amusing, the way his sight and mind were playing tricks on him. Finally, just as they were about to enter the timber, he reached out and touched Jimmy on the shoulder, pointing to the stump and whispering, "Jimmy, what does that stump look like to you?"

Jimmy raised his binoculars, peered through, slowly lowered them again, and returned his gaze to the mooser. "You wanna shoot a grizzly bear?"

"No I don't," the mooser advised him.

Jimmy nodded. "Well then, let's get the hell out of here."

And that's exactly what they did.

Judging from the way Nero had been standing there observing them for so long, if that hunter had wanted his name in the record books it would've taken only a "duck soup" shot to put it there.

Instead, the Bear God smiled and respected Nero's powerful totems.

The Island of Trees

Old Nero lived to a ripe old age. The last time I saw him was during the spring bear hunt of 1972. As before, we were hunting out of the Hungry Valley cabin. By then he must have been getting past his mental prime because he came about as close to getting measured as we ever heard.

It was an early June morning and I was guiding a fellow by the name of Bud Westgate, who was hunting for the big, dark phantom. On that particular day there were three other non-hunting riders tagging along. For some reason I can no longer recall, we were out on a rather "la-di-da" ride, more for pleasure than hunting expectancy. The three others were Julia the cook, Bud's son Jerry, and a sometime assistant guide of mine who went by the name Cactus Kind.

We hadn't gone far from the cabin, still riding along the fence line of the horse pasture, when I noticed what appeared to be a moose browsing in the brush on the north side of the valley. The distance would have been about half a mile. At that time of year in those days Hungry Valley was literally crawling with moose—we were used to seeing between 20 and 30 every day. So I didn't pay much attention to this one, other than keeping it in the corner of my eye, until I noticed something curiously different about the way this animal moved. Just before we entered the timber, heading towards another meadow, I stopped my horse and slid from the saddle.

Well, Holy Christ, there it was!

Not only a grizzly, but *the* grizzly: Old Nero. And he was right out there in the open, too. Preparing a fast war plan with Cactus, we decided that he and the other two non-hunters should remain where they were to keep an eye on the bear, while Bud and I would make the stalk on horseback. The plan was practical and made sense. To get over to where he was we'd have to go around a swampy area and cross a creek that runs high in the spring runoff period, which it then was. All that ground in the springtime is just one small step away from being pure muskeg. We all knew that it was going to be nip and tuck to catch up with the bear. We could see that he was slowly feeding his way towards a dense, burned-over area.

This was our idea: Cactus would remain on a high point of land where he could see the bear and we could see him. He would give us hand signals if the bear moved off and at those times when we lost sight of it, because we were going to have to dip down into a shallow ravine to cross the creek. It was a perfect plan, even though as much speed as possible was needed. Bud and I took off as fast as our horses could move through that muck.

Once we'd crossed the ravine, we couldn't immediately get a re-sighting of Nero, but we knew he was still quite a way ahead of us. With the ends of our halter ropes we encouraged a little more speed from our horses and headed straight for the timbered area where I figured the bear was heading. We still had a bit of a problem, though: a goddamn wire fence and the island of trees that straddled it. It took us about ten minutes to get to where, without the fence, we could have been in three or four. At that moment I would have been willing to trade my left nut for a pair of wire cutters, but seeing as there were none on offer it was the long route for us. The island of trees was only an acre or two in size, but it was big enough to obstruct our view until we circled the fence line. By the time we'd done that there was no sign of the bear.

We were able to get up onto some slightly higher ground near the island of trees, and from there we could see across the entire meadow, all the way back to our spotters. Still there was no sign of Nero. We sat there on our horses and discussed the situation for a few minutes. Scanning with my binocs, I suddenly saw our spotters jumping up and down. It looked as if they were pointing directly at us, which seemed strange. I figured they must be pointing to someplace past us up in the timber, so we rode over to the edge of the trees, looking for bear tracks that should have been easy to spot in all that mud. There were no tracks and no other signs of the bear.

The situation had my mind spinning, wondering whether I was losing my hunting skills, trying to conjure up an explanation. There was no sense even trying to hunt in the densely timbered area; it would have been impossible to approach a bear in there, much less one as wise as we knew Nero to be.

We sat dumbfounded on our horses, silently shaking our heads over being beaten again. It does not bolster a guide's ego much to be continually outsmarted by what some people consider a "dumb" animal. With thoughts like that running through my mind, I led the way back past the island of trees and along the fence to rendezvous with our spotters, who we could now see making fast tracks towards us. We met up at the creek and did they have a story to tell.

They told us that when Bud and I dropped down into the creek gully and lost sight of Nero, something seemed to have spooked him. But instead of running for the burned timber area, he had turned back towards us and gone into the island of trees. As far as any of us could tell, he was in there the whole time we were between that island and the burn. He was evidently able to maintain his nerve and keep from bolting—not just once, but both times we rode close to that island. He must have been watching us all the time, and the distance between us would have been no more than 150 yards. He'd stayed put until we headed back to the creek to meet the others. Then, while our backs were turned, he'd used the island as a screen and made a dash to the heavy timber on the edge of the valley. Old Nero had once again proved that his totem was stronger than mine.

There were many other Nero hunts, but luckily for him and me they all ended pretty much the same way. Both of us were able to bank considerable wealth simply from the hype that was created by his tracks. I banked money and Nero banked fat, because over the fourteen years that we trailed him around these hills, he was able to eat his fill from the better part of twenty head of those bear-bait horses we laid out for him. He had other grizzlies helping him with that chore, too, and it eventually became an undisputed fact that we had some of the fattest and sleekest bears in this part of the country.

Unable to tag Nero, our hunters were nevertheless able to stretch out a few of his buddies, and a couple of them had skulls measuring more than 24 inches. As far as we know, though, no other hunter in this area ever got the measure of Old Nero. Even now, more than twenty years since the last sighting of my golden partner, every time I remember something about him I still get a warm, glowing feeling of appreciation from the many blessings of our long relationship.

Poisoned Relations

During my 40 years of guiding hunters I certainly saw enough grizzlies, including Old Nero himself, to keep the hunters' enthusiasms primed. The truth is, though, our hunters were only able to tag about twelve all told, although that's not a representative statistic for the bear kill here. We always knew that local cowboys killed far more than we ever did. They had something else going for them in that respect—the strychnine they were using and, perhaps, are still using. Even though it's been taken off the market in Canada, the U.S. Department of Agriculture still gives the stuff to farmers to control ground squirrels, and we know that some of it is filtering up here.

We also know that, up until recently, our very own Fish and Wildlife Branch (F&WB) was quietly issuing ranchers cans of fish that were loaded with the same sweetener sheepherders used to use. Just how many non-target animals such as marten, fisher, and wolverine have been killed by this practice is still anybody's guess, and yours is as good as mine. You can bet our guesses are better and more honest than any rancher or government official will ever admit to.

Several years ago, when we discovered that such poisonings were still going on, we took the case to local politicians. They simply passed it back to the B.C. Department of Agriculture and the F&WB, who stonewalled us, usually with a shoulder shrug, but sometimes with outright denials. It all boiled down to the still obvious influence of common-law rulings, rulings that say agriculture—no matter where it's conducted or its viability—takes priority over wilderness and wildlife, every time.

Show me the last time a farmer or rancher was charged and convicted under the Wildlife Act. Judging from the court records you'd have to conclude these folks never poach or use poison because their names and occupations are simply not recorded in case law. Do you believe in privilege?

I do have to admit, though, that perhaps our complaints to government about the diminishing number of grizzlies in this area, for whatever reasons, may have finally twitched somebody's conscience a few years ago. As of this writing, there is no longer a hunting season for grizzlies in this Management Unit (5-03). That is a good turn of events, even though it would appear to be about twenty years too late.

The question remains, how do we control the other stuff that the authorities still tell us no longer exists?

WOLVES—AND OTHERS—
AT THE DOOR

In recent years I've begun to have mixed feelings about wolves. I'm finding it hard to understand why my opinions are wobbling—we all know the adage about the difficulty of old dogs changing their ways, and it's highly probable I fit into that mindset quite firmly. For starters, my family originated in northern Europe, where fear and loathing of wolves was taught from cradle to grave. European settlers then transplanted their attitudes to North America, and occasionally even I would believe and react to some things as I was taught to do—the customary human reaction to the presence of wolves being one of these holdovers. But over the years I've had some fascinating experiences with these strange animals, and some of the encounters still have me scratching my head.

I can't say that any of them was all good or all bad; the word intriguing seems more apt for just about every occasion. The nature of wolves has to be weighed in possibilities and probabilities. For many people, myself included, the odds in the balance seem to shift a little every time you have a new experience.

It's a bit like religion: some people are devout believers on Sunday, but by sometime on Monday their doubts begin working their way forward again. As with faith, there never will be human consensus about animal behaviour, at least until we have a proven way of communicating with each other on an even basis. Until that distant, future day, the only fair way to consider our inter-relationship with animals has to be based on that scale of "intrigue" I mentioned.

From my corner of the Chilcotin cow country, I would now like to share my own pet theories on this subject, in particular my ideas concerning wolves since European settlement in this area.

Blazing Historic Trails

To begin with, I need to nit-pick some of the early written history about this part of the south Chilcotin, especially the bits about why the first white settlers, who could more accurately be described as *drifters,* began showing an interest in this area. Most of the recent writings and verbal lore suggest that the first white settlers (or Whitman, as I call them) to stop in these parts were involved in the cattle industry. That would date back to about 1860, give or take five years. But white men were travelling through here in fur brigades perhaps a hundred years before then, and that's only the trade that's been recorded. What about those individuals and small groups who always forge ahead of the recorders? Most likely they came up through the Okanagan from the U.S., adventurers who likely were the same so-called mountain-men trappers who leapfrogged their way west of the Missouri River. Many of these men were loners who left few written records. The only traces of their passing were blazes made with iron axes, and some mixed-blood babies along the back trails.

When I arrived in this particular part of the country in 1955, there was still evidence of white settlement of a sort that must have predated even the recorded fur brigades. I'm referring to axe blazes that were made when the trees around here were saplings, but in 1955 were at least 200 years old. Those blazes were hardly visible, of course, but after discovering a few and suspecting what they were, I took my own axe and whittled into them, confirming that they really were ancient axe marks. From there I made calculated guesses at their various ages.

I discovered other signs of settlement: some handmade parts from a wooden wagon or cart, fragments I found along a meadow near Gaspard Lake. From the look of them, I guessed their age to be about the same as the blazes on the trees. My estimate in dating all these artifacts placed them around the year 1800.

I also located an old tree cache that had almost rotted away, but which left me in no doubt as to what it had once been. I deduced the probable age of the wooden relics by comparing them to other old wooden artifacts from around these parts whose age was already known. I'm certain that in this high, dry altitude and climate, items left on high ground are capable of surviving for 150 to 200 years. To back this theory up with science, elk antlers found on the surface of the ground in this region have been carbon-dated back over 1,300 years. From the various historic relics, evidence I discovered with hardly any effort, I'm concluding that wheels were in use in this area as far back as 1800, and perhaps even a little earlier. And if the wheels were here, then it's not a great leap to conclude that there were horses here, too. It's those early horses that tie this story to the wolves.

As happened everywhere that European horses were introduced, there were always a few that escaped, and others that were borrowed and traded to the Indians. Although there were not a lot of independent early explorers, the ones that were here were responsible for blazing some of the major trails that come up from the south country. These trails followed the way of fur animals, Indians, and that essential ingredient for horses—grass.

Early white settlers would have known how to make crude wagon or cart wheels, as well as winter sleighs. Common sense tells us that when these people arrived in the southern Interior, they would have made carts for hauling supplies. For a start, a horse can move a lot more in a cart or sleigh than it can on its back. Couple that to the fact that in the south and central Interior of B.C. there are miles of open meadows that would have required very little axe work, and it's not hard to see how quickly the first roads would have developed. Some to the north of the Thompson River were probably in rough existence before the first flake of gold was recorded, and long before the introduction of cattle. So as far as white settlement goes, the Okanagan, Cariboo, and Chilcotin were most likely opened up by horsemen, not by the cattlemen who seem to have taken most of the recent credit.

Horse Sense

Horses were already well established here before cattle arrived. Almost all of them, whether owned by Indians or white men, were turned loose to forage for themselves during the winter months, then rounded up the following spring. Some of these horses remained on the loose and became what the next white invaders referred to as "wild" horses, which they really were not. Free, but not wild. Once free, they became prolific, feeding on the super-rich, sun-grown bunchgrasses; it is a known fact that it took only a few years for the horse herds to build up into almost uncountable numbers. Nobody knows much about their original parentage, but we do know that horses are not very chaste. Within a short time they had inbred so much that they became big of head, small of body, and tough as rawhide. That toughness allowed them to upset the long-established food chains around here, both above and below them.

The first wild animals that benefited from the presence of these new horses were the wolves and coyotes. It seems probable that the bear population made an upward surge, too, because the horses and soon-to-arrive cattle offered all the carnivores a large and steady food source that they'd rarely had before. Horses and cattle make easier prey than deer and elk, and as I have noted from personal experience, all carnivores prefer horsemeat to beef. Watching over a dead horse, a dead moose, and a dead whiteface all lying in the same meadow at the same time, I learned that carnivores will go for the horse first, every time. The only thing that might draw them away from horsemeat is venison. For anyone in need of further proof, try this simple experiment: toss your dog a beef bone, a horse bone, and a deer bone at the same time and see which one he gloms onto first.

The point is, whatever the wild canine population was before Whitman's arrival with domestic horses and cattle, the diaries of many of the early travellers and settlers make particular mention of the noticeable increase in the coyote and wolf populations. From the distance of today, my guess is that it was the free-roaming horses that had most to do with the increase in carnivores, mainly because nobody was trying to protect them. Domestic cattle were a different matter, however, as were the horses that settlers were able to control. The thing is, wild meat-eaters rarely differentiate between prey. From this point on it's been well recorded how the war between the wild meat-eaters and humans has been waged.

Whitman's war with the wild was not just against the meat-eating competition, because some bright spark came up with the idea that if the free-roaming horses were eliminated as well, there would be that much more grass for the ranchers' cattle. The first adherents to this theory began a spotty control program that was not particularly effective. It wasn't until later that they learned how to lobby the government to control horses on a wide and organized basis, and this time their plan worked. It worked so well that ranchers not only gained *more* grass for their cattle, but they ended up with *all* of it. Along about the same time they levered the Indians off most of the land as well. Free-roaming horses were eliminated by a "dead or alive" bounty system; the free-roaming people were corralled by a Canadian concentration camp system better known as Indian Reserves. In the long term, both proved highly effective, although the bounty system on the wild carnivores took a while longer. Even today it can only be classed as a halfway measure, especially when compared to the efficiency with which horses and humans were regulated.

When the government first implemented the bounty system for coyotes and wolves in this area, it did not work all that well for two main reasons. First, they had no way to penetrate the deep wilderness that comprised much of the Chilcotin; there was too much back country for the bounty hunters to neutralize and control. For a long time it was a seesaw affair. Meat-eaters would be eradicated from a small area, but within a few years wilderness dwellers wandered down from the hills to replace them and never went back. Something will always fill up a vacuum.

Adding to the problem presented by the scope of wilderness, trappers weren't all that successful. The professional types that were most efficient when it came to capturing wolves were still mostly Indians, and they did not seem to have the same enthusiasm as their white counterparts did when it came to the theory of eradication. Perhaps that was because they had long ago—like several thousand years earlier—learned to coexist with wolves.

So even though there were steel traps, snares, and bullets aimed at the wild canines, they'd grown smart and prolific enough to stay at least level with the wild food supply. In some areas they even managed to get a little ahead of the supply, and that was when all hell broke loose. The real problem was Whitman's value system. When we eliminated the free horses on which the carnivores had built up their numbers, there came a period of time when the wolves, in particular, began looking around for a new food source. And what did they find and begin to prey on? Domesticated horses and cattle.

Sweetening the Arsenal Against Nature

Civilization was on the march. The major chemical ingredient that now brought everything more firmly under Whitman's control came from some small crystals that were derived from a fruit tree in India. Strychnine. The dictionary refers to it as a pharmaceutical medicine, but the world's agricultural community soon discovered another potent use. It went on to become the most popular and effective poison known to modern man.

Here in the B.C. Interior it was once so popular that it was sold right alongside spices and home remedies in the local grocery store. It was actually sold by the pound, too. There was so much of it around in those earlier days that it now seems amazing that so many mothers-in-law were able to survive into old age. The majority of coyotes and wolves were not so lucky.

Strychnine is a terrible poison. It seems like there is only one creature on earth that would even so much as consider using it on another animal, but it's here and we have. When used as a poison, it kills by hyping up the entire nervous system in a series of convulsions. The afflicted animal simply stretches and wrenches its body to the point of paralysis. Sometime later, and sometimes *much* later, the animal dies. My guess is that strychnine induces one of the most painful, deliberate deaths man has ever devised.

If you've never witnessed this sweetener working its wonders, this time, if only this time, I suggest you take my complete word for it. You will never want to watch or experience the feeling of being responsible for its use. It puts a giant question mark behind the meaning of the word "civilization."

The insidious part of strychnine is that it travels right down through the food chain, from the targeted victim, to the creature that feeds on it, to the next, and the next, and so on. I do not know if strychnine ever loses its toxicity, but if it does it's a long way farther down the food chain.

Amazingly, it is still being produced in vast quantities. Its manufacture should have been outlawed internationally long before any of us were born, but the depressing truth is that various government-run agricultural departments throughout North America are still distributing it, mostly for controlling rodents such as ground squirrels. When the stuff is dished out to farmers for this "legitimate" control work, it becomes oh-so-easy to pass it on to friends—other people who view most forms of wildlife as a nuisance. It makes me shudder to think of what is going on with strychnine in what we like to label Third World countries. As if Canada were superior.

The 1940s added a couple of new sweeteners to the arsenal of weapons against nature. The first was cyanide, loaded into small .38-calibre, cartridge-set guns. Called cyanide guns, these were baited so that they would fire their load straight into the victim's mouth. From a humane standpoint, cyanide guns were a bit of an improvement over strychnine: they killed in about a minute or so. Another sort of plus for cyanide guns was that whatever they killed could be found later right at the trap site, allowing the trapper to salvage the carcass for bounty or to skin it for fur pelt. On the downside, cyanide guns were indiscriminate about what they killed. Their baits could attract anything from a marten to a grizzly.

The next invention, however, was the one that finally gave man undisputed control over all members of the dog or wolf family. Known as Compound 1080, this substance, as far as I'm aware, has never been distributed to civilians. But who really knows?

In some ways 1080 is a better poison. It is about the only one that can be targeted specifically at wild dogs, coyotes, and wolves. It can kill other animals as well, such as bears, but I do know it takes larger doses to do so. By making up baits in target sizes and using them only during midwinter on frozen creeks and lakes, bears can be spared. Government poison handlers tend to be secretive about this new sweetener, and I've yet to find out how it affects smaller animals such as marten, fishers, wolverines, and the like. Very little of it has been used near where I live. When I've found carcasses in the snow of animals killed by 1080, they seem to have died without a struggle. It appears they were just walking along and then suddenly dropped dead. No sign of the struggle that always gives strychnine away. Just a dead coyote curled up in the snow.

If there is to be any justification for 1080 over the other poisons, it'll come from indisputable proof that there are no secondary victims. If this is true, then it is a big plus. The big negative may be that it is simply too goddamn effective. The agriculturists may demand that coyotes and wolves be completely eradicated from wherever farmers and ranchers want to establish wilderness-style ranching operations. If that remains the criterion for controlling carnivores, then the Cariboo, Okanagan, and Chilcotin will likely be the places where these poisonings continue until everything becomes nice safe pastures and barnyards.

A Wolf by any other Name

In 1952, when I first arrived at a small cattle ranch about 30 miles north of Alexis Creek to go to work, there were few wolves in the area. Under relentless attack by all of the methods just mentioned, the wolf population had been decimated to the point where most local ranchers considered the remaining numbers "acceptable." There were a few survivors, and their tracks told us they were travelling mostly alone. These loners posed no particular threat to cattle or horses, so the blood vendetta against them had pretty much abated.

If they came within the sights of a gun, however, there was still a bounty of $40 on wolves and $4 on coyotes, and that was in addition to whatever the pelts might fetch. Don't forget that the memory of what wolves, in particular, had recently been doing to rancher livestock was still very much alive. All types of local riflemen responded accordingly. Around the ranch where I worked for three years I never did see more than one wolf at any given time. We suspected that these surviving wolves had been reduced to catching small rodents and eating carrion. But memory lives almost forever, and the old rancher that I worked for, a fellow by the name of Jack Maindley, had many negative wolf stories to pass on. A few years earlier he'd had his worst case ever—a pack of wolves had ambushed his small herd of horses, killing six of them in one night. They had frequently tapped into his cattle herd as well.

As I sit recalling conversations with the older locals from those days, some amusing memories come to mind of the social exaggeration we all seemed to employ in our attempts to scare each other. When anybody who lived around here spoke of wolves, there always seemed to be at least three different types. When a wolf or wolf tracks were seen in the bush, where the animal was obviously not looking for a domestic dinner—that sighting was referred to simply as "a wolf." The same tracks or animals observed close to a house, yard, or livestock herd instantly got elevated to "those goddamn Timber wolves." And those actually seen doing something bad, especially the ones that are black in colour (about half around here are), were always described as "those goddamn Siberian wolves."

If you think these expressions were used only in jest, hold your sides. I can assure you that we made ourselves, and almost every newcomer to the area, believe them. I don't know how far back the Siberian expression went, but don't forget that during the 1950s we were not on the best terms with the Siberians. For some people the animosity went all the way back to 1920. Hell, we used to blame the worst of our winter weather on them, and once again there were lots of believers. Add it all up and attitudes like that make you realize how elastic our minds can become when bombarded by that wonderful tool called propaganda. It doesn't take long to become hooked into repeating the same lines yourself, so that within a short time you are overwhelmed by self-made fears.

Even though most of us are well aware of this, we still continue to use propaganda as a tool. It seems to work as well today as it did a hundred or more years ago. Its effectiveness doesn't hinge on the slightest relationship to truth, and the most wonderful part is that it's completely socially acceptable. There is no penalty for using it as long as nobody spoils the game. In the case of the wolves, the truth is they are nothing more than common, northern hemisphere, grey wolves. I believe the ones over in Russia are as well.

Stand-off in Fosbery Meadow

I've always had a sort of love-hate relationship with the local Chilcotin wolves. The variance in my feelings follows the outcome of our most recent encounter. If our meetings are distant—me sitting here looking out the window and watching them play out on the frozen lake, or even having a close-encounter staring match—I tend to allow for the warm, curious feelings I get towards them. But after occasions such as the one when they came right up and grabbed my nice, fluffy little collie off the porch and proceeded to puncture him in about a thousand places, those warm thoughts tend to be hard to conjure up for

The old Fosbery homestead at Green Mountain Meadow. It was actually homesteaded by Adam Cummings, who was a trapper. It is now owned by the Gang Ranch.

a long time. I still don't know what that attack did for the wolves, but it sure as hell killed Taffy. Times like that can make a person begin to see the plus side of 1080.

When my wife used to live here, she would become upset when she looked through the window at night to see a pair or two of those yellow, slanted eyes staring back at her in the lamplight. Not long after the wolves did Taffy in, my other best friend—Husky—and I had what I still consider to be my most thrilling wolf experience.

This all happened a few years ago when Husky and I went out for an afternoon hike to locate the horse herd. It was early December and there was about an inch of snow on the ground, with the temperature just right for enjoyable walking. The only thing I had with me were the pair of binoculars I wear as often as my hat. There had been no recent wolf activity in the immediate area, and since I no longer shot coyotes there was no need to pack a gun. After travelling about two miles, we came to a large meadow, one that has gone through a few name changes over the last hundred years. It was known at first as Cummings Meadow, then Green Mountain Meadow, and nowadays it is called Fosbery Meadow and has become a local landmark.

Anyway, upon entering this meadow I spotted the horses at the lower end. It was about two miles down to where they were feeding, and as I hadn't visited them for a while, I decided to do so then. I enjoy the company of horses and dogs, especially when we are all together. So Husky and I started across the top end of the meadow, where it's narrow, heading for a better trail on the opposite side that would lead us straight down to where we wanted to go. We were about halfway across when I noticed a movement higher up along the edge of the meadow, and when I raised the binocs to investigate, I'll be damned if it didn't turn out to be a pack of five wolves trotting along on a big cow trail. Even though it was broad daylight, they were coming right towards us. I froze, wondering just how close they would come before bolting for the timber. I didn't bother to crouch; I was sure they'd spotted me. For some reason, though, they never broke their wolf stride; they kept trotting right down the edge of the meadow. They crested a low hill about 150 yards away, then nonchalantly stopped, lined up, and stared straight at us, giving us a good once-over. Husky was busy hunting mice in the high grass and still hadn't noticed the presence of the wolves. He was only about two years old at the time and couldn't be counted to make rational decisions, so I called him over to me for better control. I was worried that the sight of wolves might trigger memories of what had happened to Taffy and that he would try to make a run for home, and I knew that a pack of wolves loves nothing better than a good chase. But it did not turn out that way at all.

For a moment or two the wolves and I stood there staring at each other—the wolves thinking I know not what; me chastising myself for not bringing a camera or a gun (I still believe at that moment I was thinking more of the camera). Those fleeting thoughts were abruptly cut short when Husky finally saw the wolves. That was when the action began.

ARR-RAAR-RAARR, he roared, and whatever it was he was saying, the wolves understood it well enough to take instant exception to his attitude. Without the slightest hesitation, four of them came bounding across the meadow and right up close to us. Have you any idea how fast wolves can cross a meadow? Well these came across in twenty-foot bounds and it took them all of twenty seconds to reach us. As they approached they were making the most ungodly racket you can imagine. Not barking like dogs or howling, but just plain roaring—a sound not unlike the one Husky had made only a few moments earlier. All the while their lips were curled up as high as they could go, and the gnashing of their teeth was so loud I could hear the clicks and snaps.

A lone grey wolf stayed put and seemed to be a lot more nervous than the four who had come for a closer look. I immediately came to the conclusion that this was a family affair, and she was the mother. The biggest wolf, a black one that had led the brigade, was by then snarling insults at us from a distance of less than 30 feet. He was obviously the daddy, while the other two blacks and a grey were yearlings. Even though they were probably a year younger than Husky, they were taller by far and acting a great deal more confident than Husky was. The big fellow was really hefty, exuding strength and sureness.

Having settled on their distance, the wolves were now constantly on the move, occasionally lurching forward to less than twenty feet away. Most of the time, however, they circled us, and I can remember thinking their movements were probably no different from the system they employed when surrounding a moose. Every now and then they would pause for a moment and use their hind claws to scratch the ground. At times it looked like there was some sort of competition going on to see who could throw the most dirt. While the dirt was flying they seemed to roar more at each other than at Husky and me, and I wondered if their behaviour was a challenge, a way of spurring each other on until one of them developed enough nerve to make the first charge.

All of this was happening so fast that it simply stunned me. The noise was unbelievable, and I was in such a state of confusion that it never even crossed my mind to turn my hearing aid off.

At the outset I hadn't given any thought to the idea of running from these animals. I knew that wolves always back down from direct human confrontation and go slinking off into the bush to hide. But even while I *knew* this to be the case, Husky had yet to be taught, and it didn't appear that this family of wolves had learned the proper order of things either.

My mind and body went into one of those states of unreality, a place where your brain keeps telling you that it will all be over soon and you will wake up to more normal reactions and feelings. At the exact same time, it is reminding you that death is as natural as birth, maybe even more so. All of this makes for a quaking feeling. To comfort myself, I tried to force myself to focus on all the stories I knew that proved how cowardly wolves are. But there was a dampener to that as well.

I kept thinking about some recent attacks by black bears, which up until 25 years earlier had no history whatsoever of unprovoked attacks on humans. After that first one in Ontario, however, there had been a yearly account of black bears hunting humans for food. Three young teenage boys had been "firsts" for a lone bear. Now I began to wonder if it was possible that somebody I knew all too well could become the "first" for a wolf attack. You would be amazed to discover just how much can flash through your mind all at once at a time like this.

By now, all thought of having a camera had vanished, but *Oh dear God* what I would have given for a loaded pistol! Religious feeling does seem to grow stronger at certain times. The cold reality of my situation was that all I had for comfort was a four-inch, folding Buck knife, and I surely did have it out, open, and ready for whatever might happen.

The wolves were still trying to outdo each other on the vocal front. Husky, on the other hand, had fallen into whimpering silence, spinning around my legs like a corkscrew, pissing on my feet one moment, licking it off the next. To be honest, I sympathized with him because I, too, was having difficulty maintaining my mental confidence. More than any form of manna from above, what I really craved was that loaded gun. Barring that, I was nearly at the point where I would have gladly allowed myself to be rescued by a posse of Gang Ranch cowboys (which could have happened, but didn't).

I began to realize that the problem was not so much wolf against man, but rather a situation of wolf versus dog. I was simply caught in the crossfire. Considering the keen intelligence of wolves, it still seems incredible that those adults dared to gamble the way they did just to settle some score with Husky. Every last adult wolf in this area must surely have been aware that humans carry guns. I doubt there are many wolves in the Chilcotin past the age of four that have not been shot at.

I could see that these animals had not built up enough nerve to make the initial charge. I could also see that the greatest danger lay in the possibility that Husky would try to bolt. Even with all the fear in his soul, I knew he would not make it more than three strides before those long-legged wolves would be on him. If that happened and he somehow managed to break free and scramble back to me, the question was, would the wolves be in enough of a frenzy by then to follow? And if they were, what then?

It seemed there must be a way of turning this ridiculous situation to my favour, but I'll be damned if I could force my mind to come up with anything that could be counted on to work. I had hollered at them, but they just roared right back at me with more noise than I could ever make. I'd tried making false runs at them in the hope they would finally panic and run, but that didn't work either. All they did was surge toward me, shoulder to shoulder, mouths wide open, snapping their teeth, and making the most ungodly roar imaginable. These surges underscored what Little Red Riding Hood discovered a long time ago—that wolves really do have huge teeth. Even the young ones have big teeth! Looking straight down the throats of four wolves that way is akin to receiving a front-row seat for the open gates of hell. Let me tell you, it's not a comforting sight at all.

At one point I noticed that the wolves had scratched up a loose rock about half the size of my fist, and I cautiously worked my way over to it and picked it up. It was not much of a weapon, but it was more than I'd had a moment before. If used properly, I had the feeling it might work.

The wolves were all lined up about twenty feet away, so I made a short run toward them and let fly with the rock right at Big Daddy. It missed his head by only an inch or two, but he never even flinched. Instead he leapt straight toward me and landed about seven feet away. To this day I can still feel my heart jumping up into my throat and almost choking off my air, and the only thought that surfaced was, "Oh, oh! This is it." He stopped there, though, and seemed to be waiting for support from the others. Luckily for Husky and me, it never came.

The three younger ones started forward, seemed to lose their nerve, dropped back a few yards, and began squabbling among themselves until Big Daddy circled back and roared them into obedience again. There was no question in my mind that it had been a very close call, and I noticed that Husky's eyes were almost crossed as he lay against my ankles, too terrified even to piss anymore. I found it hard to keep my mind on a positive tack. Other things kept coming forward, such as wondering what would have happened if right at that moment Husky had bolted, or if I'd slipped and fallen down.

The wolves acted as if they were thinking along the same lines. I could clearly sense from the communication going on between them that it was now sinking in that they'd been able to come up almost within touching distance of me and nothing bad had happened. My mind was warning me, trying to prepare me for what might happen the next time they charged, because the new look in those blazing yellow eyes only further confirmed that their intended victim's position had suddenly dropped a few notches.

And it wasn't just the eye contact that had changed. There was also a new level of intimidation, projected with renewed fury by yet more scratching of the ground with hind feet. It appeared there was some sort of rallying going on, each one working the others into a higher state of "berserkedness" for what must surely be their final charge. I can tell you with certainty, that type of propaganda works as well on the intended as on the "intenders."

The time had clearly come for the propaganda machine to go into reverse. I decided to be brazen, to charge right through the centre of them, then walk slowly to the trees. There I could find a club of some sort. All of this would simply prove the old saying was true: that in the crunch, cowardly wolves always give way to their betters.

I was not exactly scratching the ground at that point, but I made the charge anyway before I lost my nerve. It didn't turn out to be such a hot idea, either. By the time I got to within eight feet of them and was *almost* ready to kick one, they all bunched up and went into a half crouch, their ears laid back as they gave us all the verbal abuse that four wolves are capable of producing. It was enough to be extremely impressive—so impressive that their line held and ours didn't. And as Husky and I slid back to our former twenty-foot position, those wolves stood up and gave one of the most spectacular power displays I've ever seen in wild animals. All tails and ears were up, ruffs puffed up like a bunch of toads, and they danced around us like a covey of witches doing their thing at winter solstice. A couple of the yearlings became so hyped up they began calling over to their mother, but luckily for Husky and me she still refused to come over and join the fray. She was talking back at them, though, and I remember thinking that if she came forward, her arrival would probably tip the entire situation toward a fatal conclusion.

I well knew that the mother would eventually come, so whatever I was going to do had to be done before she built up the nerve. My next plan was not much different from the "charge through" idea, because I still couldn't believe that those stories about wolves always backing down from humans were not, in the end, true. If they weren't true, then why had I not heard of actual wolf attacks? I never had, and that was about the only line of propaganda that I could muster for a defence.

Instead of charging straight into them this time, I began to sidle away slowly and cautiously, always facing them. It took only a few minutes to realize that this strategy was working. Every once in a while, when they seemed to sense that something was wrong, I would simply stop for a moment until they appeared to forget whatever it was they'd been thinking. Then Husky and I would shuffle sideways again. The knife in my hand continued to offer psychological comfort, even though I knew it would be totally useless in a four-wolf attack. It probably wouldn't have assisted much even if there'd been only two wolves. Still, it was all there was to be had, and some feeling of security is a damn sight better than none. In all the tumult, an old saying came to mind that went something like this: "A shaft of cold steel can warm the heart." I can now firmly vouch for that.

In the end, this was the system that worked. The wolves moved right along with us, all the time keeping up the propaganda barrage, but sometimes it sounded more like a game of fun than the clicking of their teeth implied. They followed us along for about 50 yards, at which point we were close to the trees; then the four wolves lined up on the meadow side of us, allowing Husky and me to walk into the forest unmolested. As soon as we got there, the wolves stopped following. They stood out on the meadow, raised their noses towards the sky, and emitted some long, low, moaning howls—their way of saying goodbye.

Husky and I didn't bother to reply. The last we saw of them, they'd returned to the mother and were dancing around in what seemed to be their way of telling her all about what a great experience they'd just had. By then their ruffs were down, but all tails and ears were still up to full alert. After a few moments of regrouping, they lined out and trotted off towards Hungry Valley without ever looking back towards us again.

I knew by then that the experience was over for us, too, and I set a fast course for home, having decided to put off my visit to the horses for another day. There was an even more compelling reason to head straight for home. After the wolves were out of sight I discovered that I was soaked to the skin.

Sparing the Horses

I've had plenty of other wolf encounters over the years and have had to shoot about a dozen all told. One thing they've never done is kill one of my horses, and this puzzles me because they sure as hell have killed a lot of other people's horses around here. Several of my horses roamed loose in the upper meadows and lived to a ripe, doddering old age. They would have been easy pickings for a pack of wolves, but tracks in the winter snow told us they all but ignored these horses. Right alongside, though, the wolves would occasionally prey on open-range cattle. Why one and not the other?

Their behaviour becomes even more puzzling when you consider that wolves love horsemeat—something I discovered in the era when I served up horses as bear bait. In many cases wolves fed off the carcasses as often as bears. Figure in 200 years of easy pickings offered by the wild herds, and you'd have to wonder whether horsemeat was really their natural diet. In the Chilcotin, wolves were preying on horses long before moose, because moose only arrived here in about 1920. Since than they've learned everything there is to know about killing a moose, which I'm sure is a lot harder than killing a horse. That brings us right back to the puzzle of why my horse herd has been spared. And though I've never been able to come up with a plausible explanation for this, between the wolves and me I don't mind saying that I do appreciate their discrimination.

Caught in the Headlights

Another intriguing encounter with wolves happened recently as I was driving down a logging road near the Gang Ranch headquarters. It was 11 p.m. on a February night and I was travelling over new snow that was about an inch deep. There was no other traffic on this bush road, but I seemed to be following several fresh wolf tracks, something not all that uncommon around here.

As I rounded a corner near a place known locally as Clara's Cabin Hill, I'll be damned if I didn't come upon a big pack of wolves cavorting all across the road. With the truck lights reflecting off the snow, the entire scene was lit up like your front yard, but as I rolled slowly toward them, those wolves never paid the truck the slightest heed—even though I came to a stop about 30 feet away. They never attempted to get off the road. Why hell, if I'd hit the gas pedal instead of the brake I'll bet I could've collected the biggest single wolf kill in Chilcotin history.

Instead I simply sat in the truck and made a fast count, which turned up fifteen. I allowed for the shadows moving off to the sides of the light beam and arrived at an estimate of twenty-plus wolves—all chasing and dancing around the place, some rolling and wrestling each other in the snow, but none of them fighting. They were having the grandest old get-together you could possibly imagine, and it was obvious no truck was going to spoil their occasion.

Pairs would rear up on hind legs, lock forelegs around each other, chew each other's ruffs, and lick each other's faces. It was impressive. All of them were fluffed up to their Walt Disney best and putting on wonderful displays for each other. Their coats seemed to encompass the entire range of colours available to wolves. I was so entranced that I never thought to turn off the truck engine, but that didn't seem to bother them at all. Few paid the slightest attention to me.

Before too long, however, three came bounding up to the truck and hopped up onto the bank on the high side of the road. They couldn't have been more than ten feet away when they stopped and peered in the side window at me without the slightest sign of aggression. It looked more like they were laughing, even trying, via animal telepathy, to encourage me to come on out and join the fun. Thinking back on it now I reckon they probably meant well, but those Little Red Riding Hood stories kept welling up from the past. So I pooped the party and kept the door firmly between us. Meanwhile, the three amigos danced and chased each other around the truck for a minute or two, then went back up the road to rejoin the others. Soon the entire pack began fading off to the roadside and disappearing into the winter night. It was such a strange and unexpected experience that I sat there for several more minutes, sort of mentally pinching myself to be sure what I'd just witnessed had really happened.

Finally I concluded it must have been a meeting between two wolf packs that were on friendly terms—wolves that in the enthusiasm of their greetings had simply dropped their guards. This had allowed me to stumble into what might be a common wolf-socializing event, but one that humans seldom witness.

You may think that's a far-fetched idea, but through the window where I am now sitting typing these words I've watched smaller versions of this socializing going on in midwinter out there on the frozen lake. Here at Gaspard Lake they tend to do their carry-on-together right out in the centre, far enough in to see danger approaching from a long way off and react accordingly. Seven-power binoculars at 800 yards do a fair job of bringing them in closer, but the spectacle is not a patch on what I saw from 30 feet. What could be recorded from this window with one of those newfangled, 72-power digital movie cameras I can only guess.

Lying in Ambush

Over the years I've never witnessed wolves fighting among themselves, nor seen any evidence of it among tracks in the snow. They must fight, but it's a rare event. Around here, one of their favourite games seems to be ambushing, chasing, and killing coyotes. When it comes to an ambush, wolf tracks reveal them to be capable of elaborate planning and a high rate of success. I've never seen them catching a coyote, but I've watched a few chases across this lake and later located the aftermath. On fresh snow, the tracks are so easy to read it doesn't take a lot of imagination to guess at the rules of the game.

It appears that all such catches end in a tug-of-war, a wolf or two on each end of the coyote. From seeing several of those, it's obvious the coyote separates first right in front of the hips. With the coyote in two pieces, the wolves must have a virtual volleyball-like game tossing those parts around because the blood and guts and whatever else flies or tears apart can be found spread across an acre of snow.

One thing I've never found at a coyote-kill site, however, is any sign that the wolves ate even the slightest morsel of the victim. My guess is that they use coyotes for practice, trying out schemes they'll use later when hunting down larger prey for food. I get the clear impression that coyote hunting is simply for sport and safe training, but it could also be a way of reducing competition for the small prey food source such as rabbits, grouse, and even mice and voles.

Even big wolves will hunt small prey. They are extremely cunning, for instance, when it comes to ambushing beavers as they slide through the water chutes out of their dams. My guess is cougars spend a lot of time around those water chutes as well. When a beaver scoots down one and a cougar or wolf is waiting at the lower end, the success rate for the predator is pretty close to 100 percent. Not only does the beaver provide a fat meal—the meat is extremely rich fare— but it can be had absolutely risk free. Unlike tackling a moose or a large deer, there is no danger of wolves getting their slats kicked in.

Tempting Siberia

Something that has always tempted me is the notion of what a great lark it would be in a place like this to have a tame wolf or cougar for company. The wolf idea became extra tempting recently when a lone, young, black wolf (Siberian?) began hanging around in broad daylight. He often came right up along the fence line in front of the house when I was out in the yard in plain sight. When he spotted me out with my dog, Mac, we would all sort of freeze in position and stare at each other, sometimes for an hour or more at a time.

This particular wolf never projected the slightest aggression towards Mac or me, and sometimes he would even wag his tail when he saw us. I tried walking towards him a few times, but he always moved away at about the same pace. When Mac and I stopped, the wolf would stop. After this had gone on for several days, I noted that I was able to get closer to him. He wagged his tail more often and sometimes sat on his haunches and watched. A few times he even lay down as he watched. There was not the slightest doubt that he was curious and friendly, and I considered putting food out there for him to see how far the relationship could be advanced. If my idea was ever to be tested, this had to be the once-in-a-lifetime opportunity. At the same time, knowing he would always be a wild wolf in heart and soul, I feared what would happen if he and Mac ever fell to squabbling, something that was bound to happen eventually. My little collie would end up shredded like a coyote.

The visitation went on for a month or so. As the winter was ending I decided to end our friendship, too. A month's contemplation had let me look at it from all angles and see that more serious problems lay ahead if I continued to pursue the experiment. Besides the dog, there was the human risk. And given that he was, after all, a wolf, and that this is, after all, cattle country, when the cattle returned with the green grass the cowboys would have the right to shoot any wolves harassing their livestock. And *any* wild wolf might do that. Another dampener was knowing that wolves are listed as game during the winter months. Any licensed hunter can shoot them, and there's no shortage of hunters passing through this area in winter.

With all this clear in my mind, I had the rifle out waiting for him one morning. Sure enough, right at sunrise, here came Siberia from across the lake, his head and his tail held high like he was on parade and coming again for a pleasant stare with the natives. I let him come to within about a hundred yards of me and then hollered at him. He stopped. I hollered a few more times and he stood up and wagged his tail, looking uncertain as to whether to come or go, so I made the decision for him. I popped a bullet into the ice about 50 feet to one side of him and that's when I discovered he already knew something about guns, because he started streaking for the closest timber. Just to be sure that he would never forget about men and guns, I fired two more shots into the ice behind him.

It is possible that Siberia still lives in this valley. I can't say for certain because he has never allowed my eyes to rest on him since that day, but I suspect that he is still roaming hereabouts. Last summer, a few tourists staying here told me they'd heard what sounded like a lone wolf howling from the timber across the creek.

Siberia is not the only wolf to have grown curious about me, this place, or whatever else seems to attract them here. Wolves have wandered right up under these windows, although, as far as I know, not one has ever climbed up onto the porch. But as time goes on, that could happen. For one thing, I've stopped shooting coyotes and wolves, and since I'm the only resident of this valley for six months of the year, some other wolf or wolves may decide to become better acquainted, just like Siberia did.

On one issue I'm resolved, however. Because of too many vicious fights between dogs and wolves in this vicinity, I'll be ensuring any overly friendly wolves are kept at a respectful distance by using the same educator I used with Siberia. From here on in, a staring distance of 200 yards is plenty close enough; any closer and Mac seems to feel he has to go out and challenge them in defence of me or his food dish.

There's not the slightest question in my mind that the rules in wild areas are changing. Wild animals in general have become noticeably bolder in my lifetime, and that's probably going to continue progressively until who knows what point is reached. On several occasions during the past twenty years a pack of wolves has followed me through dense timber areas. It seems to happen most often during the winter when I'm the only human in the valley. I believe that wolves are smart enough to equate that time of year with less danger and react accordingly. Sometimes they're not just following my back trail, either. Judging from the reaction of dogs and my later study of their tracks, wolves sometimes accompany us on all sides. The dogs' raised ruffs and low growls as they stare into the thickets and smell the wind tell me that we often have an unseen escort. Bears will also trail a human that way from time to time, but it's uncommon. When they do, it's time to check the dryness of your powder because you're probably going to need it.

Trusting Cougars

Cougars are the animals I really don't trust. My first close cougar encounter happened several years ago while moose hunting in November up in Hungry Valley. I had two hunters with me and we were through for the day, returning on horseback to our cabin in the late afternoon. Since we weren't far from home we were letting the horses set their own pace, which was a slow, sleepy walk due to the weariness of the long day. The three of us were talking, our horses bunched up in single file and ambling down a timbered trail. I was in the lead, talking to the hunter directly behind me, whose name was Ken. To make talking easier, I was riding a bit side-cocked in the saddle, and as we made a turn in the trail, I noticed that there was a dog following behind the last horse, the one that Big Al was riding.

In a flash I realized that my dog was not along with us on this trip, and there were no cowboys in the valley at that time. It was a strange enough situation that I leaned out to the side to see whose dog was following us. There and then I came eyeball to eyeball with a huge cougar that was nonchalantly dogtrotting along behind as close as a trained collie, with its head almost between the last horse's back legs. As I pulled my own horse to a halt there must have been a strange expression on my face, because Ken leaned over to see what had attracted my attention.

He reacted like lightning. In one motion he pulled up, grabbed the rifle that was slung over his saddle horn, bailed off the horse, and landed on his butt in the middle of the trail—all without saying a word. Al's horse was a bit behind, and by the time it caught up, Ken had chambered a round into his rifle. Before Al or his horse could react to what was happening, Ken fired a shot right underneath them, hitting the big cat square in the chest. The force of the bullet knocked the cat about ten feet into the air. Luckily, it didn't come down on any of us. That was mostly because our horses flew into the air as well, but in a more forward direction. Luckily for Al and me, they were so weary that after about four big jumps down the trail they stopped before we became unseated.

When we tethered the horses and went back to examine our trophy, I was expecting to find a starving cougar, but it turned out to be a large tom that was about as fat as any cougar could be expected to be. No sign of disease or injury, although it did have a single porcupine quill in its cheek—one that was not infected and didn't appear to be doing any harm. So why had this big cat behaved so strangely? I can only guess that it had never had a bad experience with humans and was just tagging along out of curiosity.

Another bizarre cougar experience happened a few years ago right here in this house. My wife, Margo, was still here then, and so was my best friend, Husky, who always slept outside on the porch. Sometime after Margo and I had gone to bed and I'd drifted off to sleep, I was awakened by jabs to the ribs, shakes, and kicks that could not be mistaken for amorous affection. Before I knew it I was standing on the floor, staring into the dark in a haze. Margo was all hyped up and she kept screaming that something was outside the window, fighting with Husky. Still in somewhat of a daze, I grabbed the flashlight and headed for the door wearing nothing but a pair of slippers.

When I opened the outside door, the first thing that caught my eye was this strange-looking dog on the doormat that was in some sort of boxing match with Husky. It seemed an odd way for dogs to be fighting. Since our visitor was a golden colour, like Husky, I thought at first that it belonged to a local forester who often came to visit—his was the only other dog of that colour in the district. But as my mind began to react faster, it dawned on me that those two dogs had always been good buddies, so this noisy fight didn't make much sense.

Trespassing, picking a fight in the middle of the night, depriving me of sleep—it was obviously high time to educate the interloper and put an end to all the commotion. I stepped back to give it a good kick in the ribs and hollered as I was winding up my leg. But before I could give it the boot, this "stray dog" turned its head, which was as big as a washtub, towards me and *spit!* Well now, everything fell into place in an instant.

Since the big cats began using my yard as a gathering place, I've encouraged friends with hounds to come and bag a few. These two Nanaimo hunters, Ted "Running Dog" Chappell (left) and Ted Barsby, are old friends who have taken several, a couple of which were big as lions. That's my dog Husky with Chappell.

I aborted the kick, jumped back inside the house, and continued hollering at this unholy apparition, the whole time trying to slam the door closed behind me. But I wasn't fast enough. The big cat already had its head and shoulders inside and it was trying to squeeze the rest of its body through to follow me in. I knew I needed to lay my hands on a gun or an axe—immediately—but the axes were on the far side of the cat and all the guns were locked up. The only weapon I had was the flashlight.

I had enough presence of mind not to turn my back on the cat. I stood my ground and continued hollering, banging it on the nose with the flashlight, whose beam may also have been blinding it to some degree. By this time Margo had come to the bedroom door and, seeing what was going on, started hollering and screaming too, and that was when the big pussy decided that there was too much noise for him. He turned and nonchalantly trotted up the yard and out through the gate with his tail cocked straight up. It looked altogether to be as tall as a nine-foot fence post.

That was an unsettling experience. After it was over, I can recall reflecting on how vulnerable I felt when that cat had its head right up against my knees and there was not so much as a thin piece of cloth between its razor-sharp teeth and my dangling manhood. With a mouth like that, all it would have taken was a slight nibble. Even a slurp from the cougar's tongue might have proved disastrous.

Instead, we'd survived that encounter relatively intact, but poor old Husky turned out to have a claw hole in his neck. A few days later it became infected and the vet that cleaned it out charged $150 for the pleasure.

Like the wolves, that cougar wasn't the only one to pass through this yard. Another visitor used to drop in every winter around the first of January to check things out. This huge cat left the biggest tracks I've ever seen, although he never seemed to be interested in fighting with the dog or me. Instead, he'd do the rounds of the outhouses in the yard and piss on the doors. Margo used to get upset about that and it was sometime around then, to keep peace in our family, that I bought one of those flushing-style "thundermugs" that can be stored at the foot of the bed. I gave it to her for a Christmas present.

Bear Incursions

Another confrontation happened at this door a few years ago, but this one was with a rather large brown bear. By then I was back to living alone except for my really best friends, all of whom have four feet. On this occasion I was sitting at the counter having breakfast when I heard one hell of a commotion out on the porch. When I stepped toward the door to peer through the window and see what was going on, a large bear reared up on the other side. He was looking in at me and our noses were no more than two feet apart. Standing up that way, the bear was not only taller than me but twice as wide as well. Before I could do anything, Husky leaped in from the yard side of the porch and grabbed Mr. Brown Bear by his butt and the battle was on.

I wasn't thinking too fast that morning, and instead of running to unlock a gun I simply stood there watching the fray. Surprisingly, it looked like Husky was going to win. I could see Brown Bear was backing up all the time, until he was cornered on the porch taking swipes at Husky. It seems strange that a 60-pound dog can bluff a 350-pound bear that way, but it often happens. As I was about to snap the lock on the door, it was suddenly too late. At that moment Brown Bear leaped backwards and hit the door with his butt, slamming it open. Now the back half of Brown Bear could be seen bulging inside the house.

Once again there was no equalizer at hand, either behind or above the door where we used to keep one, so this time I didn't hold back with the kick. Bears don't move as fast as cougars, and I wound up and drove my booted foot as hard as I could right up between that bear's back legs. I must have made a good connection, too, because he let out the damnedest squeal you can imagine, jumped over the dog, and landed out in the yard, where the two of them started taking turns chasing each other back and forth through the trees. I finally got a gun unlocked and went back out to help my buddy, but by that time he didn't need me. He had chased Brown Bear up a tree beside one of the cabins. Under those circumstances, the law allows you to shoot a bear whether it's bear-hunting season or not. But this one had done no harm other than wandering into the wrong place, so I tied up the dog, got my camera out, and shot the bear a few times with that instead. Some interesting pictures came out of the whole experience, but I also got a sore, arthritic hip joint from kicking too hard. I just hope that stupid bear hurts as much as I do.

I often see that particular bear close to here, and I suspect that's because it's the same one that first showed up in the yard as an orphaned cub or small yearling. Back then it was about

This is the bear I kicked out of my kitchen. It still comes to visit, but it is much bigger now..

the same size as the dog, and I often watched them playing tag. As the bear was not bothering anything, I never bothered much with it, other than chasing it away a few times. It always ran from me and then, as far as I could tell, would stay away for long periods of time.

There was another interesting aspect to that bear, or some other enterprising bear, which began when I discovered a large hole under the cookhouse. At first I suspected Husky had dug the hole, but after a while I realized that even though he spent a lot of time staring into it, I never once saw him climb down there. Strange! Another thing that seemed odd was the fact that my three tomcats practically lived under the cookhouse until the hole appeared. After that we never saw a cat go under there again.

Then one day it dawned on me. Whatever bear was using the hole was incredibly sneaky about it because, as far as I know, nobody ever saw it coming or going. Judging by Husky's behaviour, I figure that bear must have slept there for at least two winters. And even though the hole has been there for a few years now, the toms still refuse to go under the cookhouse.

Black bears are common around here. In the summer of 1999 the yard seemed to be dripping them. One black mother brought her two cubs into the yard five times in one day, and the cubs were having a grand old time flattening my rhubarb patch and teasing my new dog, Mac MacKie. A few other blacks and browns and a good-size grizzly helped round out our summer's social life. As my friend Mike Elvin commented a few times, "These goddamn bears think they own this place," and he's probably right.

Most of the time, though, and especially during the long, quiet winters, it's the wolves who remind me that people have not yet destroyed the entire wilderness. They still come right into the yard and up to the porch railing at night, and as the years go by they seem to be getting bolder about doing so. A few times recently, when I've looked out this window at night, I've seen a pair of those slanted yellow eyes not more than twenty feet away, staring back in at me. As long as I don't move or make a noise, they will stand and look for a few minutes at a time. It's a look that can give you a warm and, at the same time, eerie feeling of tranquillity.

I feel like I'm being sent a message that is both desperate and wonderful, a message that makes a person pause and reflect. Perhaps we're telling each other that the wilderness we have known, the land that has supported us, is almost gone now. And that could mean we are almost gone, too. So at this window and door we share our message: OOOOOOOOOOOOOoooohhh.

BUCK FEVER

Judging by all the hullabaloo you hear these days, quite a few people around this country are under the impression hunters are a bit nuts. I'd like to take this opportunity to straighten some of these vegetarians out, because for the most part they don't have their information right. The truth is, only some hunters are nuts, although it also has to be admitted that a few of these have spells where they become downright deranged.

To put the foregoing into perspective, I'm going to relate some experiences I've had with both hunters and assistant guides, and believe me when I say I've had to put up with more than a few strange cases over a 40-year period. I know there are many sane hunters out there who will wish I'd skipped over this subject, because we all know the condition itself may have no solution. Nuts will always be nuts. That said, I still believe the bull should be taken by the horns because all too often this subject is dismissed in jest. When someone succumbs, though, it's not one bit funny.

I'm talking about "buck fever."

In our vocabulary that expression can now cover a lot of different mental situations, but there's no doubt that it originated in the field. Hunters of old were no different than the hunters of today when it comes to this peculiar form of malady. Buck fever has always been associated with people who become "over hyped" in the pursuit of game animals, regardless of whether the hunter is using a bow or a gun. The term applies to all those who shoot by reaction rather than after first thinking the situation through to its probable conclusion.

We're comparing reaction shooting with rational thinking, a topic that always seems more amusing when applied to other people. In my opinion, there's only one situation in which a reaction shooting should ever be considered, and that's strictly in a *you or me* confrontation. So far in my life I've never been faced with making that type of shot, and I hope I never am. There are too many question marks about the long-term consequences.

I do know that reaction shooting is taught as part of training for commando forces. A war-trained instructor once told me quite a bit about it, particularly the many known cases where people fell from "friendly" fire. I guess such casualties are acceptable in a time of war, but when hunting for bucks and bulls they certainly are not.

My First Gun

The first time I witnessed a case of buck fever—in actuality a case of *pheasant fever*—was a long time ago when I was guiding my first hunter. The experience would have been enough to cure any normal person, but a thirteen- or fourteen-year-old boy is rarely considered to be in that category, and I was no exception. The events I'm about to describe took place where I was raised, in south Surrey, B.C., about a year after my dad finally allowed me to have a gun of my own. This turned out to be a Harrington and Richardson 12-gauge, single-barrel shotgun known as a "Topper." This shotgun, which I bought brand-new for $28.50, was a strange affair to be sure. If used with low-base Canuck shells it worked fine, but when I upgraded my ammo to high-base Imperials, it was an altogether different story. When I fired I was left with the main stock in one hand and the front stock in the other, while the barrel did about three loops in the air to where I would have to retrieve it and snap the whole thing back together again. Nothing ever broke and I was never hurt; it simply flew all apart. I knew this wasn't a particularly safe condition, but I was afraid to tell Dad for fear he would condemn it. Then I would be out of the gun business, perhaps for a long time, because I knew of no other shotguns that could be purchased for such a small amount of money.

Discretion prevailed until early one morning when I spotted a pheasant almost under the kitchen window, grabbed the gun, snuck out the back door of the house, and took a sluice shot at it. As always, the gun flew apart, but I hadn't noticed that Dad was watching me from the window of the dining room. About the time I was putting the gun back together again he came running out with a strange look on his face, hollering, "What the hell happened? Are you okay?" Caught in the act, it always seemed best to tell the truth. So I did, and just as I suspected, there was a negative price to pay for doing so. I'd tried to sound casual. "Oh, there's nothing wrong. The gun falls apart once in a while, but it shoots fine." By then I had the gun reassembled and was getting ready to reload it. Dad wasn't having any of it. He snatched the gun out of my hands and exclaimed, "You aren't shooting that goddamn thing again because it's going right back to the store and those bastards are going to give you your money back." He refused to be swayed, even after I pointed out that the same gun had just put fresh meat onto our table.

There were times when Dad could be stubborn about things like that, but in the end we did get my money back. Within a few days I'd answered an ad in the *Surrey Leader* and was able, with Dad's blessing, to buy a Stevens double-barrel shotgun in good condition for $30. Now I had a better gun for almost the same price, and I was still a hunter, which was my all-consuming priority.

In those days I had an older hunting partner who could also be described as a hunting instructor. In practice it was a two-way affair because he could hunt for only three months of the year while I could indulge myself year-round. As a result, I would usually hang up more meat. This fellow went by the name of Don Turnbull, and the major reason he hunted only three months out of the year was that he had to stay home the rest of the time to make a living for his wife and two young sons. He did this by operating the Standard Oil service station across the King George Highway from our house.

As any fool can figure out, a hunter on the prowl twelve months of the year is going to learn skills that occasional hunters take many more years to acquire. Added to that is the fact that younger people lucky enough to be recruited into realms of education they enjoy become fast learners. Often, within no time at all, they even become teachers of a sort themselves. And that was how I came to be trying my hand as a hunting guide at a rather young age.

My Apprenticeship Begins

My first opportunity arose while hanging around Turnbull's service station one Saturday morning. I was busy staying out of labour's way, keeping my mouth shut, and not bothering anybody of consequence when in off the highway tools a friend of Turnbull whom I'll call Willie (not his real name since he might still be around here someplace). He was driving every teenager's dream car: a 1939 or '40 hot-rod Ford Coupe that was decked out with a couple of long radio aerials, several foxtails, and a pair of lace panties he swore he never had to buy.

I knew Willie from a distance. He was a few years older than I was, and up to that time I'd been under the impression we didn't share the same interests in life. A four-year age spread was enough to keep us apart. As Willie was tanking up his car, however, I noticed he had a shotgun-shell vest on, and it was fully loaded. So while Don was filling the tank, I sauntered over to flap my ears a bit, because it sounded like Willie was talking about hunting birds, and not the variety that usually commanded his full attention. When I got over to the car and looked inside, the first thing I noticed was that Willie had a Model 1897 pump shotgun in there, along with two unopened boxes of Imperial shot shells. To me these certainly were a lot more interesting than what normally occupied the passenger seat of his car.

That Saturday morning the conversation was on better topics too, and I quickly picked up on the fact that Willie had recently taken up pheasant hunting, although he was apparently not having much luck. It seemed he was nowhere near as proficient as he was at hunting that other type of game. As a matter of fact, it sounded like he had yet to shoot a single bird. Since Willie was a steady customer, Don was nodding in sympathy to everything Willie was complaining about—the lack of pheasants in the country, how wild the ones that were left were behaving, things like that.

It set me to wondering whether Willie was making the same mistake that Turnbull himself made. Don would claim he was hunting for sport rather than pot, and when he did that, he often came home empty-handed. Meanwhile, his hunting partner, who believed in no such malarkey, would have more birds than he did, sometimes the only ones. The difference is this: one shoots birds only on the fly; the other shoots them on sight, which often means when they're on the ground or roosting. The same went for ducks sitting on the water. In both these latter cases, shooting the game is referred to as "sluicing," something the *true* sportsman claims he'd *never* do. Not within a friend's sight, anyway!

Don Turnbull carried this subject to ridiculous ends, possibly due in part to the fact that he'd recently been delegated authority in the RCAF. It could be said that he was a bit of a teacher, or at least he fancied that he was. But as we all know, school is only in when the pupil is respectful of the teacher and of the subject he or she is trying to teach. When the teacher cannot make his theories take anchor, he might just as well be whistling in the wind.

As Don was putting the gas cap back on the car, he glanced up at me and made an obvious facial expression, a warning that the teacher within had just had a sudden awakening. He nodded at me in this particular way he had, not really a request, more like a command, and he said, "Edward, why don't you jump in with Willie and guide him to some of your favourite pheasant spots?" Before I had time to answer, Willie blurted out, "Oh God, Ed, would you?" All of this took me by surprise, especially when this older sort of peer, who had hardly acknowledged my existence before, began coming across like one of your "new-found friend" types.

It threw my mind into immediate overdrive and I was busy calculating all the positive possibilities that could evolve from doing what was being suggested. For one thing, we had just pumped a full tank of gas into Willie's car, which was almost unheard of for a teenager in 1948. If I remember rightly, gas at that time cost about 25 cents an imperial gallon, so that fill-up would have cost him over $3! For another, Willie still had money left over. To cap it off, there were all those shotgun shells lying in the car and poking from his vest. Put it all together and it was like being invited to a Royal Shoot with nobility. What red-blooded hunter could even think of refusing such a request?

Why, those assets alone would enable us to hunt and shoot all the way over into Langley, I figured, maybe even up the valley as far as Chilliwack. I was born in Chilliwack but had never been back since. Being only 50 miles away, it had always seemed like it might be worth a visit, and it now occurred to me that this might turn out to be the best opportunity to do so that would ever present itself. I can assure you there are no limits to what a young teenage mind will come up with when offered the use of a driver with a hot-rod Ford and a full tank of gas. This was surely going to be an October day to remember! Without any further discussion I nodded to both my new best friends, replying with uncharacteristic brevity.

"Sure," I said.

But first things first. I lit out for the garage and grabbed my own shotgun along with the only four shells I owned. I ran back to the car with them, but before I could even open the door, Turnbull had grabbed me by the shoulder and pushed me up against the side of the car. He made a fist and pressed it firmly against my upper lip while issuing an unmistakable *order*, which was: "Edward, today you let Willie do the shooting. ALL OF IT!" This he emphasized by sort of grinding his fist under my nose. I didn't put up any argument, but neither did I verbally agree to what was being proposed. Rather than losing this golden opportunity, I simply nodded my agreement.

Don must have thought he'd made a convert out of me because he never backed up his demands by insisting I leave the gun behind. Before he could come to his better senses, I had slid into the passenger seat and signalled Willie to take off, which he did in legendary style. When I looked back to see how impressed Turnbull was by our launch, I could hardly see him at all. He was bent over, facing the opposite direction, and trying to shield himself from the flying gravel.

Leading the Hunt

As soon as we were mobile, my mind resumed the task of sorting out the possibilities and probabilities of the day that lay ahead and of what it might produce. Seeing as I wasn't totally stupid, I decided to try some places close to home rather than steering us into the upper end of the Fraser Valley, an area whose layout I didn't know all that well. Instead, I aimed us toward prospects that had always been just a little too far away to get to on a bike; places that were maybe past the three-mile range, but within eight. I had spotted several such places whizzing by from Dad's car, or from Turnbull's, but Don would never go in and check them out because he said they were "posted." In our lingo that meant it was somebody's private land and they didn't appreciate hunters going onto it. He wouldn't even venture into those places when he knew there was nobody home to chase us off. Like I said, I was convinced that was one of the main reasons he would sometimes arrive back home from a hunt with no birds to show for it. There was no question in my mind about his attitudes—they had everything to do with the fact that his age was becoming a hindrance. Why else would he refuse to do so many other perfectly logical things? As every teenage boy knows, by the time people hit 30, most begin losing their sense of adventure as self-preservation takes over. By comparing Don's stories of his earlier life to the way he was behaving now, it was obvious that he was going through some sort of change of life. Well, that was his problem and so far, luckily, it hadn't become contagious.

That day I felt certain that things were going to turn out much differently. As Willie was peeling north down the King George Highway, I gave him a signal to turn down the road to Crescent Beach, which he did in grand style. It felt like we'd taken the corner on two wheels. After only about two miles in the car with Willie, I knew his driving was everything I'd heard it was. He could bank and spin that Ford around faster than Don Turnbull could turn an airplane. This probably had a lot to do with Willie not yet being anywhere near 30.

As soon as we cleared the area known as Elgin, we slowed down to a reasonable speed so we could get a good look into all the small clearings close to the road. Even though Crescent Beach was only three miles from home, it was an area I'd hardly ever hunted, as every fence post along there usually had one of those mean-spirited signs on it. It was pheasant country, though, and I'd been told those signs, while keeping some out, could make for game-farm-like conditions for those adventurous enough to ignore them.

I'd also heard one of my older hunting buddies mention that for someone to be convicted of a criminal offence, the game warden has to prove "criminal intent." The way this fellow had it figured, if a person could prove he was illiterate, then how in the hell was he going to be held accountable for a sign he could not read. To me this seemed like valuable information; I suspected I knew some teachers who would willingly testify that I fit squarely into the illiterate category. As a matter of fact, a couple of them had already said so—although not yet in a court of law. So far I still hadn't worked up enough nerve to give it a try.

Willie must have known the entire road was posted, too. But from the way he was staring straight into the clearings and front yards as we searched for pheasants, I began to wonder if his hunting ethics might be shaped along different lines to those of the prude that owned Turnbull Motors. Since climbing into the car with Willie, my mind had been plagued by uncertainty about how far Willie would be willing to go to bend a few minor rules. I suspected that because he was relatively close to me in age, there might really be a peer situation here that could be used to good advantage. But I could not come up with any plan for broaching the subject with him. Luckily, circumstances took care of everything for both of us.

We'd reached the midway point between Elgin and Crescent Beach and were cruising past a stand of large maple trees that surrounded a small clearing, almost part of somebody's front yard, when suddenly I spotted what we were looking for. I hollered to Willie, "There's a pair of cocks!" After jamming on the brakes and slamming the Ford into reverse, Willie took us back to where we could observe everything at a glance, then killed the engine. He reached for his shotgun as he was opening his door, but I hadn't opened mine yet because there were two obvious problems with the whole situation. First, there was a house less than a hundred yards away. Second, there was a page wire fence between us and the birds, and every post had one of those spoilsport signs nailed to it. Willie was standing beside my door by then and stuffing shells into his gun. Through the open window I quietly informed him, "The place is posted." Willie never took his eyes off the place where the pheasants had run to hide, and without looking back at me he whispered hoarsely, "What the hell, do you know how to run or what? For Christ's sake grab a handful of shells and let's go get dinner." Without another word I stuffed my pocket full of Willie's shells and slid out the door. But as I reached back for my own shotgun something twanged my mind: the memory of a big fist. At that I left the gun in the car and started immediately for the fence ahead of Willie.

My hands being free, once I got there I pushed down on the wire so Willie could do a one-handed vault over, after which I quickly followed. By then we could no longer see the birds; they had seen us coming and had run for cover under some blackberry brambles. But we knew within a radius of about twenty feet where they would be lying, and we began walking at a slow pace directly towards that spot. Within a moment we were within perfect shooting range. I'd noted earlier that Willie had loaded three shells into his gun, so I knew we were in for at least a two-bird kill, perhaps more, since there may have been birds in addition to the ones we had seen. I began wishing I'd brought my own gun after all, as this was supposed to be a buddy shoot—and buddies share things, don't they?

We crept forward until we were within fifteen yards of where those roosters had to be hiding, close enough that there was simply no sense in going any closer. I reached out, tapped Willie on the shoulder, and gave him a sign to stop so that he wouldn't blow the birds to pieces when they broke cover. As we halted I noticed movement in the brush—both pheasants beginning a running start to get airborne. I quickly stepped off to the side to give Willie a clear shot at them, but there was a deafening BANG before he even got his shotgun to his shoulder. I was almost knocked over by the muzzle blast; it left my right ear ringing like a goddamn school bell. Even in my stunned state I knew something had gone wrong, but I still wasn't sure whether I'd been shot.

As it turned out, I was okay. Barely. I had been standing just to the right of Willie while he had been carrying his gun in a two-handed "across body" position. When the gun went off, the charge shot right out in front of me and missed by no more than three feet. Nobody had to tell me that it was too close for comfort. For some reason, though, it didn't scare me as much as startle me. It took only a couple of seconds to come to my senses, however, and when I realized what had happened, I noted with relief that Willie had not, and was not, pumping another round into his shotgun to take a second shot.

Instead, he was standing there with a surprised look on his face and staring at his gun. The situation was not an easy one to respond to, but I do remember blurting out, "What happened?" Willie began quietly shaking his head and sheepishly replied, "I dunno, but when pheasants jump out that way, my gun just goes off before I really want it to."

"Were you carrying the thing cocked?"

He was still shaking his head as he answered, "I don't remember cocking it."

The answer didn't make much sense. Either he'd cocked it or he hadn't, because his type of shotgun had a visible cocking hammer and it's one of the safest designs that's ever been made. It hardly had to be said out loud how and why the gun had gone off. We were still standing there, staring at the gun that we both wanted to be the culprit, but before either of us could come up with any other explanation or even say another word, we heard a screen door slam and a woman's voice screaming, "WHO'S IN MY GARDEN? GET THE HELL OFF OF OUR PROPERTY!"

We could see the old girl standing on her porch, and she was staring straight out to where we were. It looked like she might even come out into the field. Willie reacted faster than I did. He started moving out, and as he did he said, "Oh, oh, they're home! Last one to the car takes the rap."

That had to be the signal to peel dirt, and we both took off in high lopes. I beat Willie to the fence and this time cleared it without any hand tampering. Reaching the car, I turned back to see how Willie was making out and looked on as he also took the fence without using his hands, although his jump was different from mine. Since the shotgun he was carrying had now become an encumbrance, and because he must have felt unbalanced, instead of trying to clear the fence completely in one jump he hopped up onto the top wire. He proceeded to balance there for half a second; then with one last leg-push he landed down on this side as the fence let out a loud screech. It sounded as if it might now be in need of some minor repairs, but we didn't bother hanging around to do them. The car fired up on the first try, and a second later that Ford was peeling rubber just like a teenage hot rod is supposed to do.

After we'd driven a mile or so in silence and could see that there was no one in visible pursuit, Willie turned to me and said, "I'm sorry I screwed up the hunt that way, and I'll sure as hell try not to do it again. Do you know any other hot spots close to here?"

We were already heading towards a logged-off brushy area known as Ocean Park. Some of the old clearings had always looked interesting to me. It seemed as if they were made-to-order "check out" places, and this surely had to be the best time in the world to find out exactly how good they might be.

"Sure," I replied. "Keep going straight ahead and there is another clearing down here that's just as good as the last one, and there ain't no houses close to it either." All the while, the major thing spinning through my mind was Willie's response to the previous "posted property" notices. Clearly we were coming closer together in that peer-grouping thing, and this could have nothing but positive consequences for me. I can tell you, the thrill of being on an almost-level plain with somebody as old as Willie brought my ego up a notch or two, and my mind was by now completely in overdrive.

Within a few minutes we were there and Willie parked the car well off the road. We piled out and I decided once more to leave my own gun in the car, at the same time trying to keep a veiled eye on Willie as he loaded his shotgun, straining to see whether he was leaving the cocking hammer up or down. He got it right. All the same, as we began walking down into the field I deliberately kept to his right side because he was still carrying the gun in the cross-body position.

The property we were heading into had a loose barbed-wire fence and it, too, was posted with those familiar, unfriendly signs. This time we didn't bother mentioning them, but kept marching forward as nonchalantly as we could. We'd hardly even started down the clearing when two hen pheasants exploded—as only pheasants can do—out of the tall grass. Hens were not legal game in those days, but I paused anyway because there was a good chance that a rooster might be lying back there and letting the hens take the flack before he himself bailed out. Even with their birdbrains, rooster pheasants have learned a thing or two.

These thoughts surfaced in a second as the hens rose up, but before another second could go by, BANG went Willie's gun again. This time I was almost ready for it, but in the same instant a sinking feeling went through my mind and body, warning me that perhaps Willie had shot one of the hens. Even way back then, most of the time I did try to adhere to the more common rules of the field. And the most prominent one was that female birds and animals had to be spared because only through them would there be any roosters, bulls, and bucks in the coming years. As it turned out, no real harm was done. It was another one of those cross-body hip shots—in the opposite direction this time.

Willie turned to me with a sort of twisted wince on his face. "Ah shit," he exclaimed. "I did it again!" By then we were both sure about the source of the problem. Even so we didn't say much, probably because neither of us knew what to do about it. Willie was looking glum and he didn't say a thing as he turned and began to wander back towards the car. This jangled my alarm bells instantly since it appeared he might be preparing to call the hunting excursion quits, and that was something I was nowhere near ready to do. After all, the day was still young and there were several more places I wanted to check out while I had access to motorized transportation.

Rather than risk losing the advantage, I called out, "Ah hell, Willie! That can happen to anybody. Let's keep going here and try it again."

Willie stopped, turned back to face me, and asked, "Do you really want to?"

"Hell yes," I replied. "We can't go back and face Turnbull without at least a handful of feathers."

Willie grinned, nodded his head, and stuffed another shell into his shotgun. This time he deliberately let me watch as he dropped the hammer into the right place.

We resumed walking down through the overgrown clearing, and this time I made a noticeable point of walking on Willie's off side, a little behind him. He nodded in agreement, and from then on we never had to play games with each other. We hadn't gone far before we spotted two cock pheasants on the fly. They were coming straight towards us, but landed about 60 yards away, farther into the clearing. They didn't seem to have seen us, but we could still see them on the ground because they had begun feeding in an open, grassy spot. It was too far away for a sluice shot, so we continued making our way, very slowly, towards them. I was still positioning myself far enough behind Willie to keep a good weather eye on his trigger finger. This time he was advancing as he should, keeping one finger on the hammer and the other off the trigger.

We were now within about 30 yards of the two birds, and it didn't make sense to try going any closer as we could clearly see both of them. It was already a "ducks in a barrel" situation. In addition, I could tell that Willie was getting jittery; he kept rubbing his thumb over the gun hammer, which I knew might not be a good sign. He was obviously in a dilemma about what he was going to do next. The truth is, so was I. I was wondering whether Willie had any qualms about sluicing those birds on the ground or whether he was going to turn out to be like Don Turnbull and insist that he had to shoot them out of the air, like a *true* sportsman. I sure as hell knew what I would do, and when Willie turned to face me with a questioning look, I decided to test our relationship to the limit. As this was my first attempt at actually guiding someone else, especially an older person, I didn't know how far Willie would trust or use my judgment because we hadn't discussed things like that. I knew that I'd never had an older person accept my opinions as authority on any subject, but I had the feeling this new situation might somehow be different, so I gave it a try.

I reached out and gave Willie a tap on the shoulder, at the same time giving him the "Whoa" signal. He stopped on command and his facial expression told me he was ready for the next. Just then both roosters walked out completely into the open at 30 yards and stood there side by side. I noticed Willie beginning to tense up again, so I moved back about half a step and whispered to him, "Shoot fast." This time, Willie's gun came smoothly up to his shoulder and BANG! He got both birds in one shot.

Talk about a happy hunter! Talk about a happy guide!

Willie thanked me profusely for helping him as we carried a bird apiece back to the car, and we both began to jazz each other up over our new experiences. We laid the roosters out in the trunk of the car and admired them for a while, and it sure was the right medicine to medicate the tenseness of the past hour. That was the way the rest of our day went.

We ended up getting two more roosters, both taken out of the air. Willie fired a total of three more shots; one of them was another of those little white accidents, but by then we were sort of ready for them. From watching Willie take the two out of the air, however, I could see that he was beginning to calm down to a more controllable level.

As the day was winding down and we were cruising back towards Elgin, I can still remember running the day's shooting events through my mind. Here's the theory I came up with and still adhere to to this day. The most likely reason for this type of hyper hunting behaviour is that hunters are unaccustomed to seeing wildlife or pursuing a live target and are not attuned to sudden movements and reactions. Perhaps we should make a point of deliberately positioning ourselves closer to wildlife in the off-seasons, so that we are not confounded when birds and animals do appear suddenly. If there is a cure for the fever, then this must be it.

As that day came to a close, several other things spun through my mind, not the least of which was the confirmation that I did have peer support. Not only that, but as I'd already figured out, our methods could put as much meat on the table as any of those on-the-wing shooting sports can do. And it can be done with a lot fewer shells, too.

On Willie's account, though, Don Turnbull did get his way. Of the four roosters we brought back, I hadn't fired a single shot. And we never used anywhere near that full tank of gas either. Willie probably wasted the rest of it chasing that other type of game he loved to pursue.

This little episode still seems trivial in many ways, but it has never left me. At the same time, even though there could have been serious consequences, the memory and obvious risks were never strong enough deterrents when it came to gambling on the danger posed by other people's reaction-shooting problems. In less than two years I was up here in the Chilcotin, off on a lifetime adventure of guiding hunters for a living.

Perhaps my response stemmed from the mental blockage typical of most teenagers, the stubborn belief that bad things happen only to other people. It's damn the torpedoes and let nothing get in the way! Given how common that philosophy is among young folks, it's remarkable so many teenagers survive those years—yet most of us do. Even I survived, and you know what? I enjoyed almost every moment.

By George!

Over the ensuing 40 years I was to witness several dramatic incidents of buck fever, and some of the assistant guides who worked for me saw their share, too. One that remained a negative experience right up to the end occurred on a hunting trip into Hungry Valley. The assistant with me was guiding two hunters, while I guided a third, all hunting for moose or deer. I don't recall this third hunter's name, but his face, the conversation, and the hunt itself are still clear in my mind. For the purposes of this story, let's call him George.

As was usual, the hunt began early in the morning and we set off from the cabin on horseback, hunting out into our designated areas. I led George into a large, wild meadow that was about two miles from the cabin. Two small islands of timber stand out in the centre of this meadow, but the horse trails go around the outside edges. As we were riding around the meadow's north edge we spotted a whole herd of moose—four cows and a large bull— storming out of the timber on the south side and headed straight towards us. As soon as we saw them we bailed off our horses to make ourselves as inconspicuous as possible. I snatched the halter rope from George's horse, and he reached quickly around to draw his rifle from its scabbard. Since we were a fair distance from any trees, we were in a bit of a predicament as to where to tie the horses. Modern rifles have a terrific muzzle blast, and given the sensitivity of their ears, it's a rare horse that doesn't react negatively when a gun is fired nearby.

I learned a long time ago not to trust any horse to ground hitching, especially near large wild animals or any kind of shooting. (For a ground hitch you simply drop the reins or halter rope on the ground and a well-trained horse will stay, just as if it was tied to something solid.) Every time I tried it, there was always a better than 50-50 chance I'd have to walk home.

As George and I stood there watching the moose carousing their way towards us, I was hoping that even if they did see our horses, they would mistake them for other moose and come closer. That sometimes does happen, especially during the rutting season, but this time it didn't work out that way.

The moose were about halfway across the meadow when they must have got a whiff of our scent, because they slowed down and began acting wary. The bull took the lead, trooping his harem into one of the islands of trees, and there they all stopped. We could still see them faintly, but it was too far away to try a shot, and with their heads up in the branches we couldn't tell the bull from the cows. The moose must have thought they were hidden because they showed no interest in moving farther back into heavier timber. So we all stood there for a while.

When it became obvious the situation was going nowhere, I decided we should gamble on moving. We led our horses over towards some timber where they could be tied; then I whispered to George, "Settle down into the hummocks and find a solid rest in case the moose come out and the bull presents a broadside shot." I knew that George was an experienced hunter and a better-than-fair marksman, so the plan had merit. I gave him a few additional instructions before I left, because it was going to take a few minutes to get the horses squared away.

"George," I advised, "if the moose break out while I'm gone, they'll probably come out in a line and go back exactly the way they came. If the bull gives you a standing broadside opportunity, make a try for him. But if they come out in a group, then for God's sake don't try a flock shot."

George agreed and settled down to wait. Meanwhile, the whole situation was making me nervous. I've always hated guiding hunters into a herd of animals, because once the shooting starts and the animals are running, hunters tend to lose sight of their first target and will try for any animal.

Almost every hunter I've guided has told me he had years of hunting experience, which in literal terms might be true. But the relevant fact is that most of them are once-a-year hunters, and it pays to be skeptical about all hunters until you know them really well.

Another thing I didn't like about this situation was the range, which looked to be about 400 yards. Few hunters can make a proficient shot from that distance. More often they miss or, worse still, succeed in wounding an animal that may not ever be recovered.

These moose did stay put until I returned, though, and George and I began devising another plan of attack. Since there was no hope of the moose coming any closer, it was up to us to narrow the intervening distance and increase the odds in our favour. Agreeing to this, we both stood up and began walking—not directly towards the moose, which might spook them into running too soon, but along a quarterly angle, hoping to create the impression that we hadn't seen them yet. That approach often works, and the sidelong stalking worked this time, too.

It didn't take us long to narrow the range to 300 yards, which is acceptable for a shot. It began to appear as if we had a good chance of hanging this bull up. Since everything was going according to plan, we kept moving slowly along, and we made it another 50 yards before I noticed movement in the trees. The moose were obviously growing nervous and were about to make a break for denser cover.

I stepped back behind George and cautioned him, "Okay, it looks like they are coming out. So get set."

George assumed a steady stance and sure enough, a moment later the first moose out was the bull. It had only made a few strides before George upended it with one shot—a perfect shot when you consider that it was taken off hand at 250 yards, and at a moving target. It was a well-placed shot, too. When the bull fell it was all over.

Right then I was as pleased as punch with my hunter's coolness and ability, and I was just about to reach out and give him a clap on the shoulder for a job well done. But now one of the cows began moving out, striding along at a fast pace. Before I could even raise a hand, George threw up his rifle and fired another shot, only this time he missed. He started running towards her, jacking another round into his rifle. I immediately began hollering after him and running to catch up, but he paid no attention to me. To top it off, he turned out to be a faster runner than me.

We'd covered about 20 or 30 yards in full stride before the next cow came out, and I'll be damned if George didn't fire a shot at her, too. This shot was taken on the run and had hardly even been aimed, so it looked like he'd missed her as well. I'd almost caught up when George took off after the next cow to emerge and now fired a shot at her. Again, luckily, it looked like a miss.

The rifle was empty by then, but when the last cow came out, George started off towards her, fumbling to reload his rifle on the run. We sped right past the fallen bull and George paid no heed to him whatsoever. He was beginning to slow down and I was almost up to him again, still screaming at him to stop shooting. By then I was close enough to him to hear him whimpering, "Oh God, oh God, oh God."

He managed to jack some more shells into his rifle and fired two more shots almost from the hip, but by then all the cows were so far ahead that I was doubtful if he hit anything but blue sky.

The shooting finally came to an end, possibly because George was becoming winded. He lost his balance and slipped over on the top of a greasy hummock, upending himself between two more big ones. As he fell, the rifle flew ahead of him and landed on top of yet another hummock. I jumped right over top of him and grabbed the rifle before he could recover enough to start reloading again.

George just sat there down in the hole, not saying a word. His face had an ashen look, but I couldn't tell if he was hurt. I can still remember the feeling I had of not caring whether he was or not. I stood there in silence watching him, and he continued to sit there, staring straight ahead with a vacant look. I wanted to bust that rifle over his head, but luckily for both of us I was able to control the urge. Sometimes my tolerance for such blatant stupidity is short.

Everything was now at a silent impasse. After a couple of minutes I guess we'd both cooled down a little because I reached over to help pull him out of the muck he was mired in. As he was coming up out of the hole, I quietly asked him if he was okay, to which he replied, "Yeah, I think so." We then walked slowly, side by side, back to where the bull lay. As we walked along I was watching George closely because he had a kind of zombie look about him. It was impossible to guess what he might do next.

George was still looking pale and acting subdued as we examined the bull. We hardly spoke to each other as he helped me roll it over onto its back for easier gutting. I proceeded to clean the animal. George hardly helped me with the job at all. A couple of times when I did ask for his assistance in holding a leg apart, he did so, but without any enthusiasm, and he refused to make eye contact. From all appearances, he was still in some sort of shock.

On the upside, it was a large bull that had a horn spread of 49 inches.

The dressing job over, there was still one more thing that had to be done. We had to track those cow moose far enough to find out for certain whether any were wounded. If there was blood in those tracks, then we had a bigger problem than we thought.

I walked over to where I'd laid aside George's unloaded rifle. Without asking him or saying anything, I helped myself to his belt pack, which was also lying there, because the extra cartridges were in it. George was sitting atop a dry hummock, watching me, but he never said a word as I reloaded his rifle.

I nodded to him and said, "I'll go check out the tracks of those cows to see if we have more work to do. I might be gone a while so make yourself comfy until I get back."

He only nodded his agreement, and as I started out I was much relieved that he hadn't offered to come along with the notion of maybe finishing off his own handiwork. I didn't know exactly how to tell him I didn't want his company, but I guess he'd gotten the message without words being said.

It took me an hour or so to locate all four moose tracks and to follow each one far enough along to be satisfied that none of the cows had been hit. By the time I returned to George and the bull, he seemed to have come out of his trance and we began talking quietly. I brought the horses over and we struggled to lift the two carcass halves up onto our saddle horses for the journey back to camp. What a struggle! It was a super-heavy animal, and in the middle of the meadow there was no tree limb to use for a block and tackle. Out in the open like that it's normally a job for at least three men, and four is better.

Now we get to the part that really bothered me—even more than the crazed shooting—and to some extent it still bothers me today. After we led our horses back to camp, we spent the rest of the day skinning the carcass, cleaning the meat, sacking it, and hanging it on the meat pole. When we were done we still had quite a bit of daylight left and we were obviously going to have a lot of loose time on our hands. This was only the first day, and since the other two hunters were George's buddies, they would be sticking together for the full seven days of the hunting contract. George couldn't leave even if he wanted to, because they were all travelling in one truck. Like it or not, we were stuck with each other.

Steve and his two hunters eventually returned to camp moose-less, and that evening at supper I related the entire story to them. All the while, George sat at the table with a sour look on his face, staring at his plate and picking at his food. The rest of the crew thought the whole thing was the most hilarious tale they had ever heard. By then even I could see some humour in it, but the mood of levity wasn't going to last long.

The following morning Steve and his hunters headed out before daylight, leaving George and me to kill the rest of the day doing nothing. Seeing as it might be that way for the next five days, it wasn't a pleasant situation to be in. By midmorning, George and I were into about our tenth cup of coffee and had straightened out most of the rest of the world when he finally put it to me. "When are we going to go up onto the ridges behind the cabin and try for some of those big mule deer?" he asked.

Holy Christ! I couldn't believe he would have the gall to ask anybody to take him hunting ever again. Since I had already mentally decided that he was grounded for the rest of this trip, the question stunned me. Finding I was incapable of conjuring up an unprovocative answer, I took the bull by the horns and reversed the question into a sort of challenge. "George," I said, "after yesterday I know that you aren't safe to go hunting with. What would have happened if those moose had been cattle, or horses with a rider?"

This guy wasn't going to be put down that easily, though, and he came back at me with, "Ah, come on Chilco, don't be such an asshole. You knew goddamn well there were no other animals or people on that meadow except those moose, so what harm was done? I've never shot a horse or a man in my life," he went on in a vain attempt to reassure me.

My first thought was, "God, I sure as hell hope he hasn't," but at the same time it got me to wondering if he would even admit to it if he had. I didn't trust his assurances and told him so, and for a while after that we had a lengthy and heated debate. What bothered me most was the fact that he never apologized or expressed any feeling of remorse whatsoever about what he'd done. Was this a longstanding problem he had? I wondered. And how might he be apt to react if there was no witness at his elbow? There were all sorts of questions flitting through my mind and they were not alleviating my concerns one goddamn bit.

We were becoming a bit too hot under the collar, so I finally broke off the discussion by declaring, "George, if you want to carry this thing any further, then tomorrow you and I will Unimog to Clinton to discuss it in front of the game warden or a Mountie. If they say I should take you out hunting again then I'll do it, but I'll be goddamned if I'm going to volunteer to do it without such an order." At that George jumped up off the bench, grabbed his hat, and started for the door. "Fuck you, Choate," he whispered hoarsely as he stormed out of the cabin. He went for a long walk somewhere and I noted with satisfaction that he had not taken his rifle.

That evening Steve and the other two hunters returned to camp with a moose of their own, and that tended to soften the conversation. The lighter mood prevailed until one of the hunters asked us, "What the hell did you two do around here all day?"

When George had returned to the cabin earlier that afternoon he was still seething in anger, and we had barely spoken a word to each other since. But now, with the others here as a buffer, he had loosened up to the point that he beat me to the lip, snorting in reply, "We did everything except what I thought I was paying my guide to do."

I noticed a slight wince from both the other hunters, who must have instantly realized that they'd inadvertently reopened a "no-no" subject. We were all heading into the cabin to have supper, and as we sat down I decided to try to get this thing settled once and for all—before the next morning when George might try propositioning me to take him hunting again. It seemed like the best way to resolve the issue without coming to blows was to draw cooler heads into the discussion. By fishing around for a reasonable opinion I was hoping to enlist support for my stance on the subject. But it didn't work out that way because neither of the other two hunters would commit himself.

At that point I was beginning to grow more than a bit angry myself, since in my own mind I had no doubt that my decision was based on solid ground. I can assure you I'm not a prude: I have absolutely no qualms about bending pointless rules and stupid laws into more rational directions. But there are some common-sense rules that should never be bent, and I figured this was one of them.

The whole time the table discussion was going on, my supposed long-time friend and hired hand Steve Johnson was sitting at the end of the table, chomping away on a cob of corn, taking it all in with a big grin on his face. I got the distinct impression that Steve was enjoying the predicament his boss had gotten himself into, and it was apparent that he wasn't going to offer the moral or employee support I figured was my due.

Well, if he thought this whole thing was so goddamn funny, I decided there and then that I would set him a little straighter on the subject. During a lull in the conversation I laid it on him. "Steve, tomorrow why don't you and I trade hunters and you take George up on top for a deer? You know that country better than I do. Meanwhile, I'll take these other two guys out to bring in the last moose."

Johnson simply continued grinning and chomping away on his corn, never missing a beat as he cackled back, "The day I want to be shot I'll do it myself." This was not the kind of reply or statement I was expecting, but it seemed to have the desired effect just the same, producing snickers from the two hunters and a crimson face on George. For the remainder of that hunting trip, the subject of whether George was going hunting again was never mentioned.

For the next three days, between George's long walks without his rifle, he and I spent the time entertaining ourselves playing two-bit poker and straightening out the rest of the world. He was able to wreak a bit of revenge, too, relieving me of about $50. And even though that hunting party ended up bagging three moose and two deer, better than average for a seven-day hunt, none of those hunters ever booked a hunting trip through this camp again.

Although a few other "feverish" hunters did end up shooting the wrong animal, or sometimes shot too many, George was about the worst case we ever had. The difference was that all the others were extremely embarrassed and apologetic for what they'd done. Not one of them attempted to justify his mistakes by downplaying the situation. But old George, he absolutely refused to admit that he ever did anything wrong.

Silence is Golden

Luckily, most cases of buck and bull fever are harmless, and some are downright funny. You're probably already familiar with the classic fever stories, the Hollywood-like cases where a hunter gets so excited he levers all his fresh cartridges out onto the ground while attempting to shoot the prey. In this camp, no hunter ever did exactly that, but there were a few cases where the hunter fired a shot, levered an unfired cartridge out, fired another shot, levered out another unfired cartridge, and so on until he ran out of shells.

Often this had no real impact on the hunt as the fumbling rifleman usually bagged his quarry anyway. No harm was done and, in the long term, the experience might even have been good for some people. It may have alerted them to the fact that there were times when they didn't have as strong a handle on their emotions as they thought. For any rational person, however, it must be embarrassing, especially when a friend or professional hunting guide is standing at your elbow. As I said before, when two people know a secret, it's not likely to remain a secret for long.

Stories like these make for great laughs around a jug and campfire, and we would never use real names, would we now? Of course not! To suggest that these experiences are harmless, well … that's for the most part true. Except maybe when there's a hunting guide around for a witness. From the stories handed down by my own assistant guides, you'd be surprised what some victims are willing to pay in the form of tips to ensure the guide keeps his lip zipped—at least until the hunter leaves camp. It's lucrative.

That last scenario has jogged my mind about a case involving an ex-Gang Ranch cowboy I mentioned earlier. Cactus Kind, who worked for me as an assistant guide for a while, was a good storyteller in his own right. You really need him to put all the emphasis in the right place and do full justice to this story, but I'll give you a second-rate version anyway.

As ever, we were on a hunting trip up in Hungry Valley, and Cactus had taken a young hunter out into the deep spruce swamps that run along the foot of the Hungry Mountains, which are part of the South Chilcotin range. They were hunting mostly for moose, but the hunter had tags for every type of game that was in open season. Because of the denseness of the trees and the bogginess of the muskeg, they were proceeding on foot, and on this memorable morning they walked right into the biggest mule deer buck that Cactus had ever seen. The deer was so close that the set-up could only be described as a "duck soup" opportunity. Cactus quickly stepped back behind his hunter and whispered, "Shoot!" He was absolutely dumbfounded when the hunter never raised his rifle or moved a muscle but just stood there transfixed—staring at the deer as it stared back at them.

As Cactus described it to me later that day, "I kept whispering to the stupid bastard to shoot, shoot, shoot, but all he did was stand there like a fuckin' stump until that deer must have decided it'd had enough of us and slowly wandered off into the timber. After that, the dumb bastard seemed to wake up and he turned to me and said, 'WOW! That must be the biggest deer in the country. Let's go get him!'" So they made a few circles up through the trees, but never spotted the deer again.

Cactus told us this story while the hunter was still in camp. I believe what pissed him off most was the fact that his victim— a young fellow who was new to the game—had not offered the customary incentive to keep the guide's trap shut. There went another hunter who never came back to this camp again as far as I can recall.

Getting Lucky

Another assistant guide had a rather different experience a few years later that I'm not sure should be classified as buck fever, but I'll pass it on to you and you can put your own handle on it. For the sake of possible embarrassment I'll change this fellow's name too, because even though the events were a long time ago, as far as I know he is still very much with us today. Let's just refer to him as "Lucky."

The whole thing happened out of the Hungry Valley camp during one of the years when I had to train a new hand as a hunting guide. Lucky had been an off-and-on cowboy for the Gang Ranch for several years, and as he'd let it be known that he was looking for something better, I agreed to give him a chance. An assistant guide usually earns about double a cowboy's pay, and for the right person the job is a lot more interesting. In addition, guides are often treated to free booze and, on successful hunting trips, large tips. Occasionally there are even invitations to go and visit clients later in far-off places.

In comparison, a cowboy is expected to roll out as early as a guide, but instead of a dude to impress there is only a snarly cowboss who continually threatens the hand with "work or walk" incentives. For this outfitter, hiring an ex-Gang Ranch cowboy had several advantages. Since we didn't have to orient him to the surrounding country, his training usually amounted to no more than learning a few hunting ethics and some basics on how to deal with people, particularly the stupid ones. And since in the past most cowboys were born and raised on the land, in the Cariboo and Chilcotin that usually meant they already knew enough about hunting to bluff their way through almost any questions or challenges. Rounding out these natural abilities, a guide in the Chilcotin *must* be horsy, and anyone who has survived more than two seasons on the Gang Ranch would sure as hell qualify on that point.

Lucky fit the bill on all counts, although he had never done any actual guiding. Sure, he had been hunting out of necessity all his life, but there is a big difference between being a hunter and working as a professional hunting guide. A guide has to set up hunting and shooting opportunities for others, and I can assure you that is an altogether different game than hunting for yourself. The solo hunter simply bails off his horse and shoots whatever he wants, but when guiding others the principle of *no* shooting by the guide ensures there's no race to see who gets the first shot. At least there's not supposed to be.

Some so-called guides never make the grade for a second season. Right now the B.C. government requires a minimum of two years as an assistant guide before you can become the boss Guide Outfitter. (It used to take six, then went down to three before being reduced to two—judge for yourself what it takes to call yourself a professional hunter.) Don't let anybody sell you short, because experience counts for a lot, and that comes from 40 years of guiding.

The outfitting game has plenty of pitfalls. Sometimes assistant guides become totally frustrated with their dude hunters because a lot of them are so painfully green and slow at doing things. When an easy opportunity is missed, the hunt can go on and on, sometimes ending without success, which usually means no fat tip for the guide, even though the eventual outcome was no fault of his own. One of the biggest worries for an outfitter is ensuring the assistant guide does not wind up shooting game for the hunter. That's illegal and the consequences usually end up at the outfitter's door.

Some hunters go so far as to encourage the guide to do the shooting, then rebel at tagging the animal if it turns out to be a small one. As you can guess, when a client invites a guide to help him out in this manner, there's usually a cash incentive. Unfortunately, when it's arranged on friendly terms with no other witnesses it's easy to see why the rest of the world, and more especially the law, will never know what percentage of game animals are taken this way. When enough money is involved it tends to sour the name of sport, so it behooves the guide outfitter to offer constant vigilance and training of hired hands. Legalities were not an issue with Lucky, however, as he had a bright and cheerful personality and easily grasped all the "dos and don'ts."

But there was a problem I'd never had to deal with before and had never thought to inquire about. It came to my attention on the opening night of Lucky's first hunting trip with us, when he had to go out to the House of Lords to answer nature's call. Once he'd left the cabin, one of the hunters asked why Lucky had taken his .30-30 with him. Although this area is home to most of the largest wild animals, those of us who live here hardly ever bother carrying a gun unless we're hunting. At that time I was also on somewhat neutral terms with the Gang Ranch, so there was no need to be thinking about gun protection, especially right in my own yard.

In spite of the jokes we make about it, it's a rare day when anyone meets a large wild animal on the path to the outhouses. We learn to disregard the possibility because the chances are so remote. Our vigilance grows for a while when a bear or cougar has been seen hanging around too close for comfort, but in this case none had been.

We discussed the issue in that light after the hunter raised it, but as it didn't seem to be any of our business, we let it go at

Outfitters get paid for doing this? The year this photo was taken, that hunter was paying me US$7,500 for a twelve-day hunt. I can't remember if he got a sheep or not.

that. I remember suggesting that Lucky had perhaps lived somewhere where it had been necessary to be perpetually armed, speculating that he had not yet gotten used to living in this tamer area. Ten years earlier it might have been different, because back then even I'd travelled well armed. (The threats at that time had always come from two-legged animals, not four.)

There was another possible scenario when a guide could need his gun, though in this camp we'd never had a problem with it. I'm referring to wrangling horses in the dark. In a hunting outfit run with horses, somebody has to go out each morning before daylight and wrangle the horses, because we always try to be in the saddle right at dawn. Out at our mountain camps I was usually the one to get up first, light the gas lamps and the fire, and begin making breakfast. Once the fire was going, it was time for the assistant guide to begin his day, usually with a few gulps of last night's coffee to clear his head and eyesight. He'd head out into the yard with a lantern and flashlight to locate the horses, bring them in, then saddle and feed them before breakfast. If it was a large pasture, or if the horses had been hobbled in an area with no pasture, then all of this could take a while.

An assistant guide or horse wrangler delegated this job has to have good night vision, because stumbling around in the dark can be hazardous, especially if you bump into a large, four-legged critter that's acted a bit slow about moving out of your way. When I say "delegated," I mean it, because it's a chore only a moron would volunteer to do. That may have something to do with the fact that 30 or more years ago, in the north end of the Chilcotin, an Indian kid was sent out to wrangle the horses and was never seen again.

Be that as it may, the morning after the outhouse affair I was surprised to note that Lucky again took along his .30-30 when he went out to wrangle the horses. This was not an easy item to carry because he already had his hands full with the flashlight, the lantern, the halters, and the nosebags for graining the horses. Fortunately for him, the horses were close to camp that morning and easy to find, and it didn't take him long before his pre-breakfast chores were done and he was back in the cabin eating with the rest of us.

Before the meal was over, though, my curiosity got the better of me and I asked Lucky why he bothered packing that rifle around out there in the dark. He didn't appear the least bit embarrassed by the question. He answered matter-of-factly that he had no intention of letting "one of those goddamn bears" grab him and drag him up into a spruce swamp somewhere and chew on him.

The three hunters and I all laughed, and even though Lucky was laughing as well, we quickly realized that he was dead serious about it. But considering that Lucky had been born and raised down on the Fraser River bench land, where there are lots of bears, his apprehension about them did not make much sense. So we quizzed him further.

For starters, I told him, this hunting camp had been wrangling horses in the dark since 1943, and in that time nobody had ever been attacked by a bear or cougar. Lucky was clearly not about to let himself be put down, or off, by that piece of information. He informed us that during his years working in the Gang Ranch cow camp, the older hands had told him of countless close encounters they'd had with bears, especially back here in the mountains where all the "goddamn grizzlies" lived.

I knew that there were a few cowboy bear stories that had some truth to them, but up until that day I had never met a cowboy who had been as profoundly affected by them as Lucky was, especially since none of them had happened to him. He seemed to have absorbed all those cow camp stories as God's own truth. Moreover, visiting Jimmy Seymour and me in this camp when we were regaling our dudes at night with some rip-roaring bear stories of our own (ours being all true, of course) had probably done nothing to alleviate his fear.

Lucky was a persuasive character, and he was not going to be put off by my light opinions. He pointedly tried to set the rest of us straight on the subject. "You guys may have gotten away with this so far, but someday there is going to be a 'first time' for somebody and I sure as hell am not going to let it be me." Well we had to concede that he did have a point. At least we did on that morning.

At the same time, the rest of us found this "bears in the dark" thing amusing, although it was apparent from our teasing that Lucky didn't. By that evening, as darkness was approaching, we all seemed to be keeping a weather eye on him. Other than that, Lucky was shaping up to be a good hunting companion and guide; we all enjoyed his company because he had a lot of good stories of his own, mostly of the cowboy variety.

On the second day of the hunt, Lucky and his two hunters came trooping in about noon with a nice, fat moose slung across their saddle horses. When that happens in this camp, it's customary to take time out for a celebration—if the hunters are so inclined. Since these were, we'd all become a jolly bunch of hunters by the time darkness descended. The revelry had progressed to the point where a couple of the dudes were beginning to think they were up to becoming cowboys themselves.

By mid-evening, nature was taking its course and we were taking turns going outside to relieve the bladder pressure. Every time it was Lucky's turn, somebody would comment that our "Red Indian guide" seemed to be getting greyer around the gills, and we took note that he was still packing that Winchester as if it belonged to his shadow. As the evening wore on, somebody suggested that for safety's sake the rest of us should make a habit of singing or whistling when we had to go out in the dark. From then on we did, and when Lucky caught on he laughingly agreed that it was a good idea.

In Hungry Valley, my cabin and the one that belongs to the Gang Ranch are only about a quarter of a mile apart. When the two outfits were on reasonable terms, we often visited back and forth with the cowboys. I don't remember how many drinks it took, but sometime after supper Lucky decided he'd had enough of our bear-story teasing and he was heading next door to visit his buddies. He was probably a bit inebriated by then, but not what I would call real drunk, at least not by cowboy or Chilcotin standards.

When he told us of his plans we bid him "bon voyage," earnestly expressing our hope that he didn't stumble into too many grizzlies in the bush on his way between the two cabins. His Dutch courage was built up far enough that he just laughed off our taunts. But we noted that he'd picked up his trusty partner and latched onto the brightest flashlight in the cabin. One of the hunters must have felt a little sorry for him, because he picked up his own flashlight and accompanied him to the pasture fence—a distance of about 50 yards. When the hunter returned a few minutes later, he informed us that Lucky had decided not to take the shortcut trail through the bush, but was, instead, making a wide detour out and around through the open meadow. Obviously our guide's reasoning was still functioning okay; any damn fool knows that there are not as many bears out in the meadow as there are in the dense brush.

As the rest of us settled in for the evening, somebody poured another round of drinks to celebrate the moose we were going to get the next day. We were making even more tracks in that direction when, just as I had hauled in a good-sized night log for the heater, we were all jolted out of our complacency by a loud gunshot not far away.

Immediately, each of us grabbed a flashlight and ran outside to see what the hell was going on. From the cabin door we couldn't see anything out of the ordinary, so we walked down to the fence gate and flashed our lights across the meadow. As we still couldn't see anything unusual we gave out a few hollers, but got no reply to them either. In the end we wandered back to the cabin to continue with more important things, and naturally our conversation soon revolved around the shot. We quickly arrived at the conclusion that it had probably come from farther away than we originally thought. Lucky was simply waking up his buddies, we thought, and they were all now inside the other cabin having a good old remembrance of things interesting to cowboys.

After a while our own stories were beginning to run out of steam, so we corked the cheer and turned in to bed. We didn't know when Lucky would return and it really didn't matter anyway, as long as he was back in time to go hunting in the morning. Also, as one of the hunters now suggested, it might be better for all of us if Lucky were to spend the night in the "dry" cow camp, because we didn't know how much hooch he could handle and still function the next day. That logic certainly made good sense, especially when you know and understand cowboy priorities.

Not long after we all turned in—I myself was just dropping off—the door burst open and there was the goddamnedest screech that you can possibly imagine. War whoops like that always sound more impressive in the dark, especially when they're unexpected. I leaped out of my sleeping bag so fast that I bashed my head on the steel bunk above me and it sort of stunned me. Meanwhile, the two hunters were screaming things like, "Who is it ... What the hell is going on ... Hey Chilco, somebody is trying to break into the cabin ... Somebody fire a shot out the door and scare it away." This racket was not alleviating the problem one bit. Luckily, all our guns were unloaded and my own was on the far side of the cabin, so no shots were fired. But I did have a flashlight handy, and I trained it on the doorway where most of the noise was still coming from. By then both hunters were sitting bolt upright in their bunks like I was, and what we all saw illuminated in the doorway was the wildest, bloodiest, and muddiest looking Indian that could possibly be imagined.

There was no question that it was our guide, but he was behaving in such an incoherent way that at first I thought he'd somehow shot himself with that goddamned rifle. By then I was pretty well as hyped up as he seemed to be, so it took me a few minutes of fumbling around to get the gas lamp going. All the while, Lucky was staggering around in the half-light, babbling away about a bear in a hole and geese in the sky. In the dim light it was hard to tell if Lucky was dying and preparing to follow the geese, or if he was just plain drunk. It was hard to decide what would have been better, because I could distinctly see that he was still waving the rifle around. If he was drunk, it was obvious the situation could easily turn dicey.

When I finally did get the lamp working, we could see plainly that our wild, bloody, mud-bespattered guide was not only swinging his rifle around, but in his other hand he was holding up a large, bloody-looking goose. There was no mistaking the fact that Lucky was a lot drunker than he appeared to have been a while earlier. As the three of us stood in front of him and stared at this strange apparition, I gently reached out and relieved him of the Winchester, which he allowed me to do with no objection. I noted a look of relief cross the faces of the two hunters, a look that quickly turned to real concern for Lucky's condition as soon as the rifle was out of harm's way. To our repeated inquiries he assured us there were no new holes in his body, and it did appear to be the truth. At this news one of the hunters, who had cooled down faster than the rest of us, thought to pour everybody a good-sized nerve steadier, which prompted Lucky to explain what had happened.

It seems that after he parted company with the hunter who'd accompanied him down to the gate, he'd made a wide detour out into the meadow, just like he planned to do. But it was dark out there, so dark that he never did locate the horse trail he hoped to follow to the other cabin. He lost his bearings and ended up going farther out into the meadow than he'd intended. This is a large, rough meadow with acres of big hummocks that have deep holes in between them, and it soon became difficult for him to stay on his feet. The smooth-soled riding boots and extra couple of drinks he'd had before leaving our cabin were probably not helping matters much either.

Lucky's eyes grew round as saucers as he described what happened next. "All of a sudden something tripped me and I fell into a deep hole on top of the flashlight, breaking it. I forget if the gun went off when I fell into the hole or when I tried climbing out of it, but when it did let go, something hit me so hard that it knocked me back down into the hole again. Holy Christ, Choate, I thought for sure it was a bear, but while I was trying to get away from it, it didn't feel like a very big one. I tried pushing it back up out of the hole so I could find my gun and get ready for the cub's mother. It was as sloppy and slippery as hell down in there, and for some reason I couldn't reach my rifle up on top. So there I was, fighting with that goddamn small bear and hoping like hell you guys would come out and help. Finally I did get the goddamn thing thrown out of there, and that's when I found out it wasn't a bear at all but this goddamn goose!"

By that stage the rest of us were laughing so hard we could hardly stand up or see straight, and the medicine seemed to have calmed Lucky down again, too. So we helped him get cleaned up, and one of the guys even grabbed the Winchester and escorted him to the House of Lords to be sure he never got lost again.

It makes a person wonder about the mathematical odds—Lucky stumbling blindly into that muddy hole on a black October night, accidentally firing a single bullet into the sky, killing a migrating Canada goose he could not possibly have seen, and then having it fall directly on top of him. But there was no doubting that it sure as hell had happened! And even though it scared the wits out of our trusty guide, it added a great deal of hilarity to the stories that came later. To this day, though, I still can't remember whether we ate that goose.

Unfamiliar Action

It's fortunate that no instance of buck fever in our camp ever drew blood—human or livestock. When we had cases of totally careless gun handling, the cause was always those "once-a-year" nimrods who hadn't taken the time to familiarize themselves with loading and unloading their rifles—either people who'd recently purchased a new gun, one with a different action that they weren't used to handling, or folks who'd switched from their trusty old bolt-action standby to an auto-loader. Those goddamn auto-loaders, sometimes referred to as automatics (which they aren't), are the most dangerous guns a hunter can bring into the bush, especially when he's unaccustomed to their action.

Of the few gun companies that still make and sell automatics as sporting guns, the most popular is Remington. I'm referring here to large calibre rifles, not shotguns or .22s. All auto-loading rifles have what is known as a cocking lever that sticks out of the side of the gun. Since we usually hunted on horseback, the gun was carried in a stiff leather scabbard fastened to and slung over the side of the saddle. Though hunters don't usually carry their guns with cartridges loaded into the chambers, the magazines are always loaded. When these autos are slid into a scabbard, especially a stiff one, the cocking lever is often forced back, opening the breach. Then when the gun is withdrawn from the scabbard, the motion pulls the cocking lever closed, which in turn chambers the first round. That's the way the action works. If the hunter isn't familiar with these mechanics, or simply forgets to check (the once-a-year hunter again), he'll now have a fully loaded and cocked rifle in his hands without even knowing it. Thinking that the chamber is still unloaded, he may finger the trigger and BANG! Only luck or fate controls the flight direction of that bullet. I saw this happen several times, and I can assure you it was a rude awakening for the guide, the horse, and the hunter. It's almost enough to make a guide think about taking the cure—and head off into other trades.

The other scenario happens simply from loading and unloading auto-rifles—especially in the dark. A lack of handling

Typical young rams from Churn Creek, before they begin fighting and broom their horns.

A hunter who got what he came for.

This California bighorn from Churn Creek, B.C., is a typical broomed older ram that will never be a full curl.

Our biggest deer ever. Its "weighed in" weight, which was only the skinned carcass in the background, was 342 pounds. Estimated "live weight" would bring it up to about 600 or 700 pounds.

115

The photo at top left shows the hoodoos at Sheep Flats in Churn Creek Park. Lower Churn Creek (bottom left) is now a B.C. Protected Area, a new designation that I do not trust politically. I recently heard the Minister of Forests say the reason the government never elevated this area to full park status was because it might someday want to put a "resource extraction" road down through the centre of it, to access the wood and minerals in upper Churn Creek area. So what is protected? I hope that someday the long-proposed

Spruce Lake area and Big Creek Provincial Park will be tied together with Lower Churn Creek to make a large national park. And if we go that far, then why not tie it in with the provincial park surrounding Chilko Lake, which would make it a "world class" park. This couple from Germany (top right) hunted with me on three different occasions and shared the feelings of glory in what is now the Churn Creek Protected Area. Here (lower right) I'm looking for bighorn sheep from Table Top overlooking Churn Creek.

proficiency or plain inexperience is usually to blame. We'd be heading out on a morning's hunt, usually mounting up in the dark, and these dude hunters would, for some reason, begin fooling or fumbling around with their auto-loading rifles. Inexperienced with the action, they'd inadvertently chamber a round, touch the trigger, and again, BANG! This happened right in front of the cabins a few times as they either slid the gun in or out of their scabbards. Some hunters even blew the end out of their own scabbards.

In over 40 years it's amazing that not one horse or man was ever shot. It sure as hell wasn't because of skill! I think the auto-loading rifle should be declared a non-sporting gun and returned to its intended use—as an assault weapon. These guns may have a place in the military or survivalist's arsenal, but they sure as hell don't belong in the bush with sport or meat hunters. Any time a hunter arrived in this camp with an auto-loading rifle, we knew instantly that we probably had a dude hunter on our hands, and I mean that in the fullest sense.

To round things out, here's a short, humorous, and certainly educational field experience I had with a seasoned moose hunter. This older hunter usually used a trusty old bolt-action rifle—the safest kind made. Before he left his home in the U.S., however, he ventured into a sporting goods store where he met a salesman who was clearly the *absolute* authority on moose hunting in Canada. This salesman convinced the old hunter that he'd be wasting his time coming up here with anything less than a new auto-loader. He'd need fast backup shots to keep from being knocked on his ass by a charging wounded moose, the salesman reasoned, or by grizzly bears that ambush hunters in the dark spruce swamps. Right!

The old boy bought the rifle, tried it out a couple of times, and thinking that he had it all figured, packed up and came here to get a truck full of meat. There we were, first morning out, not having gone far, when out in the centre of a pothole meadow stood a large bullmoose that showed no sign of having seen us yet. We tied our horses to trees and walked to the edge of the meadow to within 150 yards of the bull. The hunter cranked in a round, and just as he put the stock to his shoulder he must have touched the trigger, because the gun went off pretty much out and over the bull. He missed by a mile and within the next two seconds had fired four more rounds straight up into the air. Unused to the action, his finger had frozen on the trigger; every time the gun went off it automatically chambered another round and the hunter inadvertently pulled the trigger again. When he finally got it to stop, the old fellow stood there for about five seconds with the most stunned look on his face, then took the rifle by the barrel and flung it as far as he could into the meadow.

This was rutting season, so the bull wasn't as spooked as he should have been; he simply stood there watching and listening throughout the entire fiasco. Seeing the moose move off a little way but stay within easy range, I ambled over, retrieved the rifle, and tried to hand it back to the hunter for reloading. But he wouldn't even touch the gun, said only that he never wanted to see the goddamn thing again.

He sagged down onto a hummock, and there were tears running down his face as he recounted his tale of being conned by the salesman. "That son of a bitch cost me the only hunting trip I can ever afford up here," he blubbered. He still refused to touch the gun and told me that his hunt was finished. All he wanted to do was go home. So I slung the scabbard and rifle onto my horse and we went back to camp.

He went fishing for a couple of days after that, and when I offered him a better rifle to try hunting again, he just shook his head. He was actually going to leave the auto here for me, but the evening before he left I went out and hid it in his pickup truck under his other gear. We never heard from him again and I never discovered whether he used the rifle on that salesman after he got home.

In my view, the only way to reduce these buck and bull fever cases is through more frequent human and animal contact. I believe that the more contact there is, the less likely it is that wilderness wanderers and hunters will over- or under-react in these situations. There is absolutely no sense toying with yet more government regulation. We are dealing here with the infinite variety of human emotions, which are, in the final analysis, impossible to predict.

Most people afflicted with this sort of fever know they have it and should, therefore, take personal responsibility for controlling it. For those who cannot control themselves, I can only hope that they're honest enough, especially with themselves, to take whatever safety precautions are necessary— even if that means some have to hang up their guns.

Likely the best way for hunters to become used to being around large wild animals is to diversify their bush skills. I'm willing to offer odds that by making a point of doing some wilderness wandering during the off-season, the mental hype will wear down to a controllable level after several close encounters with large animals. Some hunters argue that they cannot get enthused about wandering around in the bush for no possible gain. These are people who simply *must* bring something back with them—whether it's a head or a load of meat. They must have a material reward for spending their time out here.

For those to whom mental memories are not enough, I say consider the alternative of photos. With one of today's zoom-lens cameras there's absolutely unlimited opportunity for bagging unprecedented quality wildlife pictures. Some of my most cherished memories and experiences have come from close encounters with these wild creatures, and I'm beginning to notice that close observation of wildlife affects many of my friends the same way—and that's saying something!

For some hunters, a few pleasant wilderness sightings will have the beneficial effect of nudging them toward giving up the blood hunt altogether. We must all realize that throughout most of the world, especially the western world, attitudes are changing. But because I know how rewarding it can be, I'm not advocating that all hunters give up the hunt—only those who feel doubtful about what they're doing. My feelings swing both ways. I do know that coming across wildlife in a non-confrontational manner and leaving it in the bush as it is found does seem to give a person a strange sense of tranquillity.

KEEPING THE TROOPS
FED AND OUTFITTED

When present plans or memories of older mountain trails begin to overcome a person's better judgment, the first thing that always comes to mind is food. Whether you're getting ready to go again, or sitting around staring into the fire and remembering, food always seems to take precedence over all other priorities. If you doubt this, wait until you're contemplating your next wilderness excursion, then I defy you to try bypassing the food issue for more than twelve hours. You see, the reality of trailing out centres around food, mostly. Everything else is incidental by comparison. Accordingly, I'd like to share a few tales about grub that have lodged in my memory down through the years.

Other than meals missed, the first memorable meal preparations in this camp date from the time I was working as head guide for the previous owner here, whose name was Tex Braatz, long gone now, but hardly forgotten. Tex had set me up with a roly-poly hunter from New Jersey who'd made the serious mistake of booking into a horse outfit—a mistake because there wasn't a horse in the Chilcotin that could have packed him for more than an hour. If this fellow was going to hunt moose, then he should've booked himself on with a riverboat outfit. Since we weren't into that end of the business, the only way to give this fellow a wilderness hunting experience was to lead him on foot. So that's what I was doing.

This dude had a fancy name that I can barely recall, but I do remember that Tex said he was some sort of bigwig back where he came from and that he had a title that went something like So & So the Third or Fourth. Tex asked me to treat the fellow with the respect any *good* Canadian would show to royalty. Right!

Each morning I loaded him into an old farm wagon that we pulled with a Ford tractor and hauled him up as close to the moose pastures as we could go. Then we'd hike from there. It was a reasonable plan all right, but that fall the moose were none too cooperative. The few we were seeing were all too far away to shoot at. After a few days the Third or Fourth was complaining about his sore feet, and as the hunt was turning into one of those bloodless affairs, early one afternoon he asked me to take him back to the Gaspard Lake base camp so he could rest up for a day. I raised no objection. Sore-assed and sore-footed hunters tend to be hard to get along with, and there's nothing like a day in camp to bolster their spirits. Back to base camp to visit Tex we went.

Upon arrival, we explained why we had come back early with no game. Tex nodded and invited the Third or Fourth to come into the cookhouse, where he proceeded to make a scene out of lacing a big pot of warm water with a pound of salt and then setting it beside the cookstove. (For sore or blistered feet this brew really works.) After we got the Third or Fourth well settled down, Tex broke out a bottle of Crown Royal whiskey, which at that time was a "Canada only" beverage—it could not be had in the U.S. except through bootleggers. The Third or Fourth was duly impressed, and a nod and a wink from Tex told me that I was to lay the stuff on well and keep the party as jolly as possible. Bartenders like Tex and me had a good working relationship that way, and as the afternoon progressed it became one for the Third or Fourth, one for us, a double for the Third or

Fourth, another for us, two more for the Fourth or Third, and another for us. And so on.

Pretty soon Tex had to ante up another bottle because we discovered that the theory of alcohol tolerance having something to do with body weight was probably right. That first bottle had gone down like it was simply an appetizer. The bottom of the second succeeded in producing a pretty good glow, though.

While we were indulging this way, Tex had been cleaning a pile of veggies and I'd had the job of browning a pile of meat, all of which Tex was getting ready to throw together to make one of his famous hunting camp mulligans. The Third or Fourth had been watching all of this, informed us that he'd never had a stew or mulligan in his life, and said he was really looking forward to the meal. As a matter of fact, he'd been watching Tex so intently, and his questions were so pointed, that I got the impression he was mentally recording the entire procedure for future reference. I'm sure he must have been a connoisseur of fine food, as from his appearance it seemed he'd never missed a meal in his life. When he laughed, his body jiggled like a well-endowed woman not wearing body supports. Truth be told, not many people like the Third or Fourth have ever made it out to the Chilcotin bush.

By now we had all this food piled up on plates on the counter, and Tex was sitting beside the Third or Fourth, regaling him with some of his Second World War derring-do exploits (he had some real zingers). In a lull between stories, the dude asked Tex when he was going to start cooking the dinner. Tex never missed a beat, nodding toward the foot bath and telling the Third or Fourth, "Just as soon as you're finished soaking your feet in the stew pot." There was a slight double-take from the Third or Fourth, but he never said a word as he lifted his feet out and nodded to me to take the pot away, which I did. Tex handed him a towel and I took the pot outside and drained it, not rinsing it out or washing it but taking it straight back inside so Tex could do so with hot water. But that's not quite what happened, because as soon as Tex got his hands on the pot he started dumping all the mulligan ingredients into it and immediately set it on the woodstove to cook. By that time the Third or Fourth was slowly lacing up his boots, and as he watched Tex prepare this concoction he had a strange look on his face, but he never said a word.

All he did was nod to me to give him a refill, which I did, and before I could step back to return the jug to the shelf, the Third or Fourth grabbed it from me and doubled the load in his drink. He actually drained the second bottle, and Tex had to set another up on the counter. For the remainder of the evening the mulligan was never mentioned directly again, although I noted that the Third or Fourth never took his eyes off that pot.

A short while after dark one of the other guides, Norman John, arrived back home with his two hunters and we wasted no time bellying up to the table for supper. You can be assured that Tex had once more done full justice to his mulligan's legendary reputation, because everybody at that table had at least two or three full helpings. When the meal was over and we were sliding our chairs back, the Third or Fourth nodded towards the empty mulligan pot and remarked to Tex that it was one of the best meals he'd ever eaten. Well now, by God, that was no exaggeration either.

Hungry Jacks

Before we leave Tex out in the ether I'd like to describe the other meal he was famous for, and that was his breakfast. How are you with "Hungry Jack" pancakes? I don't know if they still make this concoction, but his were made from a ready-mix pancake formula available in 25- and 50-pound sacks down in the States. Tex had at some point mentioned that the stuff was cheap; I guess that was the reason he smuggled it into Canada by the half-ton load.

As far as pancakes go, there was nothing much different or wrong with the Hungry Jack variety, but when you have the things with every meal for more than a month, they do become a bit boring. That was the silent opinion of the hired hands, but some of Tex's clients tended to get set off by them after the third day or so and Tex, being the sort of high-class chef that he was, didn't take too well to criticism of his cooking. The only variation with Hungry Jacks was what we poured onto them. Some days it was jam, which wasn't bad; some days when the shelves were empty it was bacon or deer fat; but mostly it was corn syrup. Well, I happen to like corn syrup, but after a year or two it also can become boring. Oh yes, when we camped close to a fishy lake or stream the bacon and deer steaks were sometimes supplemented by trout, and those sitting next to the cookstove were able to saturate their Hungry Jacks with fish oil from the fry pan. Yummy!

Like I was saying, Tex didn't stand for any complaining. One morning we were all up in the Hungry Valley cabin with a hunting group from Tennessee. Tex was cooking breakfast, one of the other guides was out wrangling horses and saddling them, and I was busy setting the table and being a sort of second chef to Tex. One of these Tennessee hunters was becoming owly and peevish about not having bagged his moose yet, and for the previous few days he had been nit-picking almost everything he could detect was wrong with our operation. Everybody else was up and dressed, but this big fat bastard was still sitting in his sleeping bag, and you could tell from the downturn of his mouth that he was looking for an excuse to lay it onto somebody.

Breakfast was almost ready—Tex had a huge stack of those pancakes and a platter of deer steaks ready to go—when I suddenly remembered that the syrup was still stored outside. I went out and brought in two bottles, setting one on each end of the table. Nothing wrong with that, or at least I didn't think so until Tennessee called over to Tex and informed him, "Hey Tex, I won't eat those goddamn pancakes again unless there's hot syrup for them." As usual Tex never missed a cake flip as he turned to me and said, "Okay Slim, there'll be one less for breakfast." But it was Tennessee who backed down, eating his pancakes with cold syrup and never having the nerve to complain about my coffee making again, either.

A Tin-Can Cook

A year or so later I bought the operation from Tex, and then I became the head chef. That was a new experience, not just for me, but also for all the poor hunters, hands, and riders that I experimented on. I can assure you right now, though, that I never poisoned or otherwise killed a single one of them, even though I do remember a few who declined some of my culinary concoctions.

When I first started in the outfitting business, money, or the lack of it, was an almost daily problem. Of course, one of the easiest places to adjust your expenses is on the grub bill, and almost every new outfitter makes the mistake of trying to use that spot to straighten out other problems. I don't know why we insisted on cutting back at the table, especially given there are so many age-old sayings warning against it. Sayings like "The road to a man's heart is through his stomach" and "A well-fed hand is a happy hand." After 40 years in the hunting and trail business, I can now promise the world that those sayings are the absolute truth. No matter how wild and tough the day may have been, a well-fed and well-watered client will always detect the true rainbows in the operation. As for the hands, even if their paycheques are slow to come or occasionally bounce, as long as they feel that they are well fed, they too will stick by the boss until things are somehow rectified. But if any of them feel that the table's too lean, then it can be zilch for the outfit and they'll take you to the brink.

When I started out, we never attempted to use much fresh food. Most of our meat came out of a can and all of the veggies did. Sometimes we packed spuds into the mountains, but more often it was rice, barley, and macaroni. All of the fruit was canned too. Of course every tin-can cook has his own favourite recipes. Until I got married in 1960 my favourites were corned beef out of a can, kernel corn out of a can, and Cheez Whiz out of a jar. I would pour them into the same pot and heat the whole mess until it was all melted and mixed together, to be poured as a cream sauce over rice, macaroni, or potatoes. Even if I do say so myself, it wasn't a bad mix, but Steve Johnson used to refer

The camaraderie of camp life is the main reason people still relate to bush life. It used to be part of male bonding, but in the past twenty years the girls have come out to join us, and that is not a bad situation. Left to right, Ray Marsh, me, and Ken Osborn in 1998.

The Great Cariboo Trail Ride 1997 camp on Green Mountain Meadow. I'm obviously offering my rendition of local events to the trail riders, who organize out of 100 Mile House and often come to Gang Ranch country. Photo supplied by the guy with the high forehead.

to it as "slumgulian goulash." This had to be about the worst-sounding label Steve could come up with, but I noted that he often used the same formula himself.

In those earlier days we did occasionally have fresh meat, because I made it clear to the hunters when they arrived that I expected them to donate the hearts, livers, and tongues of any game they killed. In those days we always had a moose or deer down by the third day, and often we took one on the first. Even so, that menu could be tough on people who didn't eat "gut meat," and there are quite a few of those. Another fresh meat source was grouse, and I've yet to meet a hunter who doesn't like it. Most of my guides took to carrying a .22, and when the morning big-game hunt was over we'd grouse hunt our way back to camp. There were lots of grouse in the hills during the 1950s, '60s, and '70s, but during the '80s their numbers declined and haven't really recovered much, so they're no longer a reliable food source. There are almost no rabbits in this area; as a matter of fact I've never eaten a wild rabbit in my life.

As the years went by I learned the value of upgrading my food, especially after I ventured into the summer trail-riding business—that type of rider doesn't have the same stomach strength hunters seem to have. When I started feeding our hunters the same style of food, well, some of them figured they'd finally found heaven. I certainly noticed that it took a lot of the grumpiness out of early morning wakeups and unsuccessful hunters alike. The major reason I started out as a tin-can cook was the prohibitive cost of hauling fresh food into the hills: it doesn't keep like cans and dry goods, which means more trips to town and overall higher operating expenses. I'd made the mistake of trying to keep hunts and rides as cheap as possible, so I'd been catering to that type of clientele. But there came a time when I gambled at raising rates and supplying better food. That turned out to be a good business decision. Even though I lost most of my former clients, the new ones were a different class of people and, in most cases, a lot easier to get along with.

In later days I also learned to stock up with an extra cache of booze. I usually didn't supply that sort of thing to my clients—since the average hunter likes to imbibe a few at night, most would bring their own supply. That was fine at the beginning because most of them also shared it generously, but you'd be surprised at how often the hooch ran out before the end of the hunt. It was usually about the seventh day of a ten-day hunt or the ninth day of a twelve-day hunt.

Let me tell you a little something more about that. When the hooch runs out and glumness takes over during the table conversation at night, I can tell you that you have an education coming if you've never witnessed such an occasion. Right about then, though, when the generous outfitter returns from a short excursion to the supplies and lays a 40-ouncer on the table, he's acquired buddies for life, regardless of hunting success.

I rarely had a supply of tobacco in the hills, as having never used tobacco of any sort I tended to let those types suffer it out in their own world. Both of my wives were smokers, however, so when we were close to camp some of those clients did find solace and a fresh supply. There's only one type of person in this world worse than a dry "alky" in the bush, and that's a smokeless smoker. Believe it or not, the smokers ran out more often than the drinkers did, and it has always amazed me how stupid smokers can be that way. For example, the guy knows he has a one-pack- to two-pack-a-day addiction, so what the hell does he do but arrive out here for a ten- or twelve-day trip with a carton of cigs, which is ten packs. Now you try figuring that one out, because I've never been able to. I'd rather be in the bush with a dry drinker, even when there's no hidden supply, than with any smokeless smoker I have ever met.

On the food side, the major upgrade I finally made was supplying fresh meat. It's not legal for a guide to kill a deer or moose for "camp meat," even though I knew that there were other camps that gambled on those legalities. Some got caught and some got away with it. Of the former, you'd be surprised how many were turned in by their own clients or hired help. It all goes back to that adage I mentioned earlier: "When two people know a secret, it won't remain a secret for long."

For the outfitter who gets caught, it can be a damned expensive gamble, so we avoided taking the chance. True, wild big game, or "The Queen's Beef" as the older homesteaders used to call it, is good eating, but so is "cow meat." All my life I've had a taste for beef. After living in the centre of the biggest ranch in these parts and watching 4,000 or 5,000 of these critters wandering past the front gate for six months of the year, they finally did tickle and tease my craving enough to go back to eating beef again. Perhaps it was also because I might be a sucker for advertising. I used to see bumper stickers all around the country that advised us to "Eat More Beef."

I began to get into beef in a big way. For the last ten or so years that I was in the trail business, the first thing on the list for the coming menu was a hindquarter of the best beef available. Setting up camp at the end of a bush road as far along as we could get a truck or Unimog, I'd simply hang the beef in the full quarter in a fly-proof sack. After that I'd simply whack away at it on a daily basis any time I wanted meat. When I packed into the higher hills with horses, I'd cut the meat into smaller hunks so it would fit into the pack boxes. And that wasn't the only meat we took to the hills. I'd pack along a large ham, at least two roasting chickens, a turkey if Thanksgiving or some such event was coming up, ten pounds of breakfast sausages, and a slab of bacon. To that I added an estimated week's supply of fresh veggies. Then it was back to cans.

At the end of this chapter I've included a couple of reliable grub lists; using either one I never once ran out of food. I take a certain amount of pride in that statement because it's a known fact that this camp had a reputation for doing exactly that before I took it over. Everything would be gone except the Hungry Jacks! There were other camps in B.C. with a similar reputation, and to my way of thinking that has to be the stupidest case of poor planning there is. All an outfitter has to know is how many people he has to feed, multiply that by the number of days they're

Margo Choate serving up a "man-sized" beef steak that I had cut off a hindquarter that hung from a tree just outside the tent. Our clients and friends were always much impressed with this style of living.

We'll have to invest in bigger frying pans at Gaspard Lake. These trout are 19.5 and 17 inches.

Gang Ranch buffalo near Gaspard Lake. You may not know it, but buffalo and elk meat is the finest there is. Well, a fat moose is up there too.

going to be out in the hills, allow for two or three extras in the event of visitors or bad weather, and there you are.

I was often accused of using another source of meat as a camp supply: buffalo. But the truth is, I never fed any such thing to a single client, even though they often encouraged us to do so. This was at a time when the Gang Ranch had a herd of about 200 half-wild buffalo rampaging around here, and the goddamn things became a nuisance to anybody who owned a fence. I remember that they tore my horse pasture fence down on at least five occasions, but no Gang Ranch personnel ever came up to repair it. Alleviating the problem through the kitchen was sure as hell tempting at times, but as I say, we never fed anybody buffalo—even though it is a desirable dish. Before those buffalo were finally taken out of here, some of the bulls were ranging as far as 200 miles from the Gang Ranch, and rumours I believe suggested a few neighbours did snipe some. As of the year 2000, however, there are no more buffalo at the Gang Ranch or in my freezer. As a matter of fact, none ever was stored in my freezer.

Measuring your Firepower

When it comes to rifles, hunters will never tire of seeking advice from guides about the "best" gun calibre to use. After standing at the elbow of hundreds of hunters over the years and closely observing the performance of both the hunters and their guns, I've accumulated some educated opinions on this subject. The first and last word is that there is no "best" calibre for all game, but there are, indeed, a few that come pretty close to the mark. The rule of thumb is to fit the calibre to the animal you are most likely to be hunting. It's stupid to use a .243 on an animal as big as a moose or elk, even though I suspect that many have been killed that way. Few hunters want to talk about the game they've only wounded, however, and that would cover a lot of moose shot with a .243 or lighter calibre bullets. A .243 will work well on deer and sheep, even though I don't consider it to be the best for them, either. The .243 and some high-speed .22s are excellent on animals like coyotes and wolves, especially if the

The horses are all packed for the trail ride.

Chilco in the lead, heading out on the trail in 1982.

These trail riders remind me of an old song that went "Three foxy young riders came prancing along." These three are Barb Akerman, Sheila Wagman, and Charlotte Akerman at Gaspard Lake in 1996.

A summer romance is in the making for Brigette Schlee at Relay Creek during a 1983 trail ride.

135

hunter wants to blow them to pieces. But with the true big-game animals that around here start with sheep, goats, and mule deer, the .270 is only surpassed by the 7-mm magnum. For those same animals, a .30-06, a .300 Winchester, or a .308 loaded with 150-grain bullets will also perform well. The main difference between the .27-calibre and the .30 is in the gun's weight and the power of the recoil; the .30s tend to jump a bit more. On the other hand, I don't recommend the .270 for moose, rarely for elk or bears, and *especially* not for grizzlies. For some reason the bullets of that calibre don't seem to have the knock-down effect that all the others do. I do know this camp has lost more wounded moose to the .270 than to all the other calibres put together. I also know that a lot of hunters will howl "B.S." to that statement, but I have watched it happen time and again.

For the hunter who can handle the recoil of the big .30s, they might be a better choice. There's a much wider selection of bullet weights—right from 110-grain plinkers to 220-grain, short-range, deep-penetration bullets that in their own range will knock down anything in North America. Most of the .30s work best with bullets ranging in the 150- to 180-grain weights. There are some bigger .30s, like the .300 Weatherby, but they have quite a kick, too. In my estimation those rifles are made way too light. I'd go so far as to suggest that Weatherby rifles have ruined more marksmen than they ever benefited; the recoil can be so bad that after a few attempts many hunters develop noticeable "flinches" when they pull the trigger. And after you've been "scope ringed" by a Weatherby, you may be carrying that flinch back to a lesser calibre gun and not shaking it for a long time. (Scope ringing happens when the shooter has his head too close to the scope and the recoil splits an eyebrow or causes concussion.) I've seen a .300 Weatherby calibre adapted to heavier-barrelled guns, like Winchesters and Remingtons, and that tones down the recoil a lot. But I still tend to consider the .300 Weatherby altogether more gun than needed in North America. The .338, and the old .375 Holland & Holland, developed for medium-size African game, are unnecessary too.

My recommendation is this: improve your skill at getting within closer range of the target, then make a better shot.

There are some other calibres worth considering, such as the .30-30. It has killed a million moose (and wounded quite a few, too). It's okay at its favoured moose range, which would be less than 150 yards, and for deer no more than 175 to 200 yards. A much better calibre in roughly the same range is the .300 Savage, a gun we don't hear much about anymore. I consider it to be one of the best youth or women's calibre rifles ever made, mostly because of its reasonable recoil and surprising killing ability. Once again, I wouldn't advise stretching its barrel to more than 200 yards for moose and no more than 250 for deer. Up to 200 yards, though, it's a guaranteed better moose gun than a .30-30 or even a .270. For some reason, the Savage cartridge at its preferred range will up-end moose like nothing else in its class. For moderate ranges there is nothing wrong with the .303 British, either; it's completely comparable to the Winchester .308, but it's just that there's never been a wide selection of rifle actions made to accommodate the calibre. It's almost like the choice is Enfield, Ross, BSA, or nothing.

I'd like to finish this subject off with my new and, probably, last little equalizer, which is a new Winchester calibre model that's chambered for the .356. The reason I bought this untested gun recently is because my old .30-30 is getting on (manufactured in 1910), and it was beginning to jam once in a while. This can be a pain, especially if the need to use it is urgent. I got this new "knock-about gun" to carry as a close-range backup when guiding hunters. It's light, fast, easy to use, and a horse outfit needs something to terminate serious injuries on the trail. Have you ever tried cutting the throat of an injured horse? Well, I haven't either and I never want to have to—so there will always be a place for a trail gun. So far this rifle of mine has yet to draw a drop of blood, but since its recoil is obviously heavier than the 30:30, I'm prepared to take on any animal on the North American continent within its modest killing range of 200 yards. That said, my own hunting rifle for all game—my all-time favourite—has always been the tried and proven .30-06.

Newfangled Gear

Packing up and heading for the hills nowadays is a lot different from what it was 30 or 40 years ago, so many new gadgets are available today. Some are useful, some are frivolous, and, of course, a lot are salesmen's junk. The good stuff amounts to lightweight tents and sleeping bags, mitts and padded gloves that are actually warm in cold weather, entire lines of propane lights, stoves, heaters, and freezers. But there's still room for improvement, especially in the propane equipment.

I am referring mostly to those small, disposable propane bottles. They're undoubtedly handy, but with all of the wilderness awareness info circulating today I'm astounded that disposable bottles can be manufactured and sold. It seems like they should've been banned long ago and replaced with refillable types, but I don't believe any outfit makes them yet in a container weighing less than five pounds. I dislike the fact that disposables are discarded so carelessly in the bush and, being so durable, will still be lying there more than a hundred years from now. The same can be said for flashlight batteries. Since rechargeable batteries are readily available (and have been for some time), it seems like it's time to ban the manufacture and sale of the disposable kind, especially the ones made specifically for flashlights and radios.

The other long-time bane of the bush that you come across everywhere is the aluminum beverage can. My guess is that these discards will last more than a hundred years, too. This compares to the tin cans that rusted away inside of 50 years or so, depending on the amount of salts in the soil. Of course, the worst material is glass. It's so durable we don't even know its precise life expectancy.

Many people are beginning to pick up cans and bottles for recycling, and that's a good thing. But there are way too many who don't, and I think that has a lot to do with the lack of financial incentive. A nickel or a dime has little value today; some folks

Boys and men used to be the ones who headed for the hills instead of the towns, but times seem to be changing. I see more boys deliberately tying themselves to the towns and many more young girls are coming out here to enjoy and partake of the wild green. If only I was twenty again!!

consider them nothing more than a nuisance. Why return a can or bottle for something that's only going to wear a hole in your pocket? It's time we made container deposits more realistic.

Among the useful innovations, new lines of outdoor clothing have come a long way, even though some of the older stuff is still with us and my guess is it will be for at least another lifetime. As far as I can tell, nothing is as durable as wool and silk. Wool coats, socks, pants, and undies (if you can stand the itch) have never been beaten, except in weight. My favourite hunting coat is still a wool mackinaw, and in cold weather I wear a pair of wool pants over lighter pants. There are newer, brushed, wonder materials on the market that in the bush are just as quiet as wool, but so far the stuff is very expensive. Between you and me, I suspect I'll keep using wool to the end.

The new style of imitation fleece used in liners is mighty handy, too. From this point on there's no need to get overly cold while out there doing your thing in the bush. The one material that I caution everybody about is nylon, especially in coats or snowsuits, as it doesn't breathe well and tends to make a person sweat. The perspiration turns to clammy coldness when you come to a standstill, and in dire circumstances that can be deadly. I'd recommend nylon shell-type suits and coats only for stationary activities, like riding a tractor or snowmobile. If there's any chance you might find yourself walking home, then you'd better have something else to fall back on.

Every outdoor person's list should also include a few pairs of light, wash-and-wear gloves. Cotton, wool, and silk are the best that I've seen. I even recommend them for year-round use because you'd be surprised how cold your bare hands can become when you're trying to handle rigging in a summer sleet storm. Store your gloves in the bottom of your saddlebag and use them as needed.

Very few people bother to bring up-to-date maps into the back country. In B.C. these can be purchased at most survey offices and a few sporting goods stores. If you plan to be off the beaten track, for God's sake don't depend on free maps supplied by the Forest Service and some tourist operations. Those things are notorious for being inaccurate. The better maps can be had for a reasonable price and are worth every penny when you go off-road.

Of course a *full* lighter is a must, and a compass that really does point north will help anybody exploring new country or taken by surprise in fog or storms—whether they think they know the area or not. I've known a few guides who wandered around in stormy weather for a lot longer than they intended, looking for the tethered horses they thought would be easy to find again. One fellow I know couldn't locate his horses for 24 hours after the weather changed. Embarrassing, to say the least! As I remember, his hunters never gave him the customary tip he felt he was entitled to. Differences of opinion and values, I guess.

I once hired a guide who couldn't walk a straight line to save his soul from hell once he'd entered the bush out of sight of known landmarks. Every time he tried, all he did was walk in twenty-minute circles. At least he never lost his horses.

For trailing out on horseback, there are now some well-designed pack saddle outfits that weren't available when I started out in the 1950s. Most of the pack rigging in those days consisted of the old "sawbuck" pack saddles and a scattering of ex-military stuff. The military rigging was usually well made, but the sawbucks were as likely to cripple a horse as not, because a sawbuck is only a good saddle when it's custom fit to a particular horse. A poor-fitting sawbuck pack saddle will saw its way into a horse's back, and no amount of padding is going to help. Most military pack saddles that I have seen are made with flexible paddles. It was from these designs that the newer generation of civilian pack saddles were designed, and they were long past due for invention. For some reason the saddle makers of the world had focused almost their entire energies into improving riding saddles, ignoring the pack rigging. Perhaps it had to do with what was being packed—the difference between dead weights and human asses. Another thing that could have accounted for the lack of interest was the fact that, up until recent times, pack horses were held in low esteem and their price was gauged accordingly.

All that began to change when the horseback tourist and dude ranch industry began to flourish, which has been pretty much in my lifetime. When I began buying horses I assumed every horse for sale could be ridden and usually tossed a saddle onto it to try it out. Once ridden, the next question was "How well does this horse pack?" In my estimation, a good pack horse or, better yet, a dual-purpose horse is as valuable—even sometimes more so—as a plain old saddle horse.

Another thing the packers have in their favour now is the wide selection of pack boxes and pack bags that have replaced the old kerosene can boxes that were covered with raw cowhide. Some of these new boxes are made from the plastic wonder materials of the space age, and some show up with foam insulation for packing frozen food. Years ago I made some of my own out of wood and Styrofoam and they added several days to frozen meats. Although I've yet to use them, these newer designs look to be a big improvement over anything I've seen before. So the packers and pack animals are enjoying a resurgence, and my guess is that in parts of the world like the Chilcotin they're back to stay for a long time. No matter how far our vehicle technologies advance, there will never be anything quite like packing up and heading out with a string of horses and mules. The feeling of travelling in this manner will be one of mankind's last touchstones with the green earth that's so rapidly disappearing. It's the same out on the water; powerboats will never completely replace the canoe.

Trading Tips

In addition to better equipment, there are many new back-country food products available, and some of them are more nutritious and longer lasting as far as shelf or storage life goes. Of course there are many traditional items that may never be surpassed— like rice, bulk dried fruits and veggies, juice powders, jams, and honey—but some new products are really tasty. I'm referring mostly to the freeze-dried stuff and some pouch foods, the ones that you simply drop in boiling water for a few minutes and *voila,* they emerge as a ready meal. Most of these are expensive, but last time we used them they worked out to about $10 per head for a large meal, which compares favourably to an average restaurant meal. You need to beware of the advertised portions of those pouch dinners the first time you use them, however, because some of them claim to contain enough for two or three servings. Maybe that's true for those on a diet, but after a long day on the trail a two-person dinner for one is more realistic.

Solving the problem of food storage also calls for some ingenuity. Most of the stuff that didn't keep on our trips was spoiled by freezing, which ruined some foods and permanently altered the consistency of others. I'm not going to attempt to guarantee that the information I offer is absolutely safe, but I will categorically state that the methods described here have proved successful on many occasions. Furthermore, I hereby record that I have never poisoned a single soul. Even I've survived right to the brink of becoming an OAP.

I'm not aware of any dry food that spoils from freezing. However, you should be sure your storage containers are dry and mouse- and rat-proof. Be wary of using cardboard: some foods will pick up the taste if left for too long. Even cocoa containers, which are usually made of cardboard, will eventually transfer that "blah" taste. When storing for longer periods, say a couple of years or more, put dry foods into more durable containers. Ziplock bags are a wonderful invention, and so are all the heavier plastic containers designed for reuse.

Now we come to tin cans, which are "if and but." Canned meats made of the pure thing keep well for many years. Mostly we stored corned beef and canned hams. Some we stored in remote cabins where winter temperatures go down below -40, and they were still useable twenty years later. I've never seen a can containing those meats swell and break. Even so, always watch for rust on the inside of the can if you suspect it has been frozen. If there's any sign at all of rust, *then for God's sake do not use it!* Sardines keep so-so; they're useable, but they go soft. I've used them hundreds of times. Canned fish, especially salmon, goes soft, too. I've tried every variety but the flesh is too mushy to recommend. Jams and honey go sugary, but you can return the honey to normal consistency by placing the open container in a pot of warm water. If the container is made of tin, boiling water will do the job faster. Most jams and marmalades remain sugary but are still useable. Canned mushroom soup keeps well, as does canned beef soup with no veggies in it. Avoid storing any canned soup with veggies, as the veggies always turn soft—some beyond even what *I* would use. The same goes for most canned veggies. The only ones I recall remaining stable are canned tomato paste, kernel corn, green beans, and stewed tomatoes, which are okay in stews and chili, although the tomatoes do tend to go watery. Canned pork and beans is out. So is canned milk.

All this writing about food and meals reminds me of an amusing event, although when it happened it wasn't all that funny. I'd been back in the hills for a while and when I arrived home at Gaspard Lake, my wife at the time had an impressive dinner waiting for me. (There's nothing like long separations to bring the best out in people when they get together again.) I'd been travelling all day and was as hungry as the horse that had been packing me, so I really tied into this meal. Now this was a real meal. No hunter's mulligan this time, but several courses of the best she could conjure up (and she was a good cook). The table came complete with candles and all the trimmings.

I was almost finished and beginning to feel topped off when I stuck my foot right into it. "You know, hon," I said, "that was a great meal, but you shouldn't have gone to all the bother because I was so goddamned hungry I would've eaten the ass out of a skunk." Apparently that wasn't the type of reaction she was hoping for, because she slammed her fork down onto the table and, staring at me with blazing eyes, exclaimed, "You know, feeding you is about the same as feeding someone else's dog!" I can assure you the remainder of that evening's conversation stayed in memory for a long time.

Ah well, as promised, here are the food and supply lists I used on dozens of occasions for later rides and hunts. These lists are the result of 40 years' accumulated experience, and I don't remember ever running out of food up in the hills; more often we returned with supplies. I suggest using these lists as a guideline, adding and subtracting according to your own preferences. One system that works well is to divide all the food into daily packages before loading it onto horses or trucks. That way you don't have to go rummaging through all the boxes every day.

I always make room for a mobile pack kitchen consisting almost entirely of black, cast-iron cookware. It takes one large pack horse to carry my kitchen, but at day's end I can assure you that everybody appreciates that hardware. For one thing, and it's an important thing, black iron is virtually indestructible. When food gets burned onto black iron you can use any type of pot scrubber you want and you won't damage it (in really bad cases, steel wool with creek sand is about as good an abrasive as can be found). If the pot has been scrubbed down to silver iron, it needs to be "cured" again. That's a simple operation. All you have to do is put it back onto the stove or open fire, get it good and hot, then add a tablespoon of cooking oil and slosh it around in there. When the iron is hot it absorbs the oil, which gives the pan another slick finish and inhibits rusting. No aluminum or steel in the world will take the punishment that black cast-iron will handle.

Because of its weight, black iron isn't recommended for backpacking. If your trip is going to be a horse affair, make sure not to overload your saddlebag or bags. Consider what the horse is going to be packing. This is especially true for anyone who weighs more than 180 pounds. Some outfitters no longer allow saddlebags on their horses, and I was often one of them. We ended up setting a weight limit of 220 pounds for riders fully dressed. For riders who weighed more than 180 pounds, no bags were allowed other than a small sack to hold a camera, gloves, and bug juice, with maybe a light raincoat tied behind the saddle. (In front is better because the kidney area is the tenderest place on a horse, and that's right under the back end of the saddle.) Kidney swelling or open surface sores mean that somebody will be walking home leading an unburdened horse. Think about that. A sore-backed horse is no accident: poor padding, too much weight, and poor riding ability usually bring about the condition. Poor balance in the saddle, and that refers to both supplies and rider, is a killer. Achieving good balance is the most important aspect of trail packing and riding.

When you're catering to several people in a pack outfit, a few other basic tools are necessities. Here's a list of items I'd recommend taking along: a bow-saw of about 30 inches, a sharp saddle axe, regular pliers, needlenose pliers, a hammer (or use the back of the axe), a small coil of wire (for tying who knows what), a small roll of strong cord, a flashlight for each person, extra bulbs and batteries, a waterproof hat, and, for horse wrangling in wet, frosty grass, a pair of rubbers—unless you like having wet feet all day. We always carried everybody's rubbers in a separate gunnysack. In addition, take along a 30-inch duffel bag (hockey equipment bags are perfect) that will hold all your personal gear, including a sleeping bag, a pocket knife for each person, bug juice, and a shovel. The shovel is for making fireguards and digging small holes—when travelling in a group it's each person's responsibility to cover his or her own tracks. We leave the shovel in plain sight, with the TP stuck on the end of the handle. That way nobody forgets to take the shovel when they go for a nature walk. Oh yes, don't forget to take a heavy burlap-type bag for packing garbage out of the woods. Burning cans and bottles in a campfire and leaving them there is no longer legal. Aside from the law, there are also some pretty good social reasons for avoiding this practice.

On the next two pages are the two grub lists that I personally guarantee. I can safely say that nobody who relies on them will ever return hungry—unless they reject the cook's methods. One is for a trail trip with horses; the other, longer one I used when trucking to the end of the roads. On my last truck camps we even hauled in a full-size propane fridge, which proved to be a great asset.

You'll need the extended list of items when hunting from a seasonal camp. I usually provisioned mine for the duration of a hunting season, or at least for a long hunt or campout. From this list I would also equip my guides or myself for overnight spike camps, either on foot with a backpack or with minimal gear tied behind our saddles. Although planned as a list to feed four people for fifteen days, I remember we often fed visitors from it and still never ran out of food.

Trail Innovations

There's another item I recommend and claim as a personal innovation. How are you at eating out of a frying pan? I don't mean eating out of the pan you just used for cooking bacon, but a fresh one instead of a plate. How many times have you sat around a campfire on a cool evening or cold morning and

The Horse Trip List

(Feeds three people for ten days)

10 lb. spuds (or equivalent in rice or macaroni)

3 lb. onions	4 cans tomatoes
5 cans corn	5 cans green beans
5 cans peas	4 cans tomato paste
5 cans soup	Dry soup mixes

Lunch meat
Hamburger, chicken, ham, smokies
Quick meats: bacon, sausages, steak

6 dozen medium eggs	8 loaves bread
Crackers	1 bag pancake flour

1 syrup in plastic bottle
A few pouch dinners, just in case

4 containers margarine	1 container jam
1 containers ketchup	1 container mustard

Salt, pepper, and spices
12 cans milk (or powdered)
Cheese and/or Cheez Whiz

3 lb. coffee	1 small tea
10 juice powders	2 lb. sugar

Desserts, cookies, or canned fruit
Oranges and apples
Chocolate bars (for lunches)
Nibblings—trail mix, etc.

1 soap	1 roll aluminum foil
1 roll wax paper	1 cooking oil or lard
Ziplock lunch bags	3 rolls toilet paper
4 rolls paper towels	

And don't forget 1 sack of horse pellets for pet wrangle horse! Or prepare to walk home. (While on the subject of walking, your best trail boots might not always be the full riding type, but more likely a pair that you can walk and ride in. A light pair of camp shoes is handy, too, as is a pair of rubbers—unless you're a weather gambler.)

The Big Trip List

(Add and subtract according to your own druthers)

10 lb. flour	10 lb. sugar
50 lb. spuds	1 jar Miracle Whip
8 lb. onions	1 large jar mayonnaise
10 cans tomato paste	3 jars salad dressings,
15 lb. rice, usually instant	1 container vinegar
5 lb. macaroni	2 jars mustard
10 cans green beans	2 containers ketchup
10 large cans tomatoes	2 garlic powder
12 cans kernel corn	2 jars HP Sauce
6 cans mushrooms	1 large jar pickles
Greens from garden	Salt & pepper
20 canned soups	15 lb. margarine
8 dry soup mixes	2 containers cooking oil
15 lb. bacon	6 packets yeast
10 cans luncheon meat	1 package bran for cooking
1 hindquarter beef	2 large containers jam
3 roaster chickens	2 large containers honey
10 lb. sausages	1 jar peanut butter
1 large ham	2 containers syrup
4 cans tuna	1 container corn starch
10 cans sardines	1 container baking soda
4 blocks cheese	1 container baking powder
15 dozen eggs	6 cake mixes
2 jars Cheez Whiz	Several boxes cookies
15 loaves bread	2 boxes chocolate bars
2 bags pancake mix	2 rolls aluminum foil
1 large box crackers	1 roll waxed paper
20 small cans fruit	Toothpicks
10 lb. apples	10 rolls toilet paper
Box of oranges	10 rolls paper towels
10 lb. coffee	1 small box Tide
1 lb. tea	Meat sacks and 50 lb. fine salt
1 jar instant coffee	for hides. (If bear hunting,
24 cans milk	100 lb. salt)
1 jar Coffee-mate	25 lb. dog food

watched helplessly as the food on your tin or porcelain plate congealed to hard fat? After a pack horse threw a fit and broke all our plates, we learned to eat off the extra frying pans that survived the calamity. It turned out to be one of our better moves.

When you sense that your food is beginning to lose its culinary appeal, simply set the pan back close to, or on, the campfire until everything warms up again. Right about then the world begins to look and feel better. I took to packing one aluminum frying pan for each person in the party, preferably with lids as they help keep out fly ash and, in the summer, flies as well. Light stainless steel is probably best, but it costs more. The next time you go camping, pack a ten-inch frying pan with your personal gear and learn to ignore the laughs of your buddies who think they're still too goddamned sophisticated to use one themselves. I can absolutely assure you that your food will be a hell of a lot more palatable than theirs. I have even adapted this system for use here in my house, especially when I am "batching," which is most of the time nowadays.

Here are a few dos and don'ts for the ride.

Do: Plan dinners to be quick and simple, such as meat with rice or spuds and one veggie. After three days on the trail, especially if it's a hunting trail—when days can be long and miles longer—you become more weary than hungry. Summer trail rides and days are not as long and leave more time for cooking. A summer ride is usually ten to fifteen miles per day or about five hours. A fall hunting ride can be as long as twelve hours a day and cover 30 miles, although that's rare.

Don'ts: Don't bring bulk juice or milk. Don't bring large eggs, as vibration from the horse pack will often break them inside their shells. If you're hunting, don't forget to bring good quality meat bags (not cheesecloth).

That's how we travelled and ate in the bush.

One Last Tip

In more recent times I met a local hunting party that had a useful innovation of its own. The idea is for hunters to forego the big early morning breakfast in favour of an earlier, larger lunch. As they saw it, hardly anybody enjoys eating a big meal at 4 a.m. Instead, when they arose in the morning they had a fast cup of coffee, perhaps some cookies or a piece of cake, made a lunch, and then headed out into the dark meadows to await daylight. Now this all makes sense from every direction; the only way I could improve on the system was to make up the lunches the night before. It's too easy to be forgetful when trying to force yourself awake at those early hours.

It's not as if a hunter has to wait until noon to eat his brunch, anyway. Most game animals retire shortly after daylight, and it's not very productive for hunters to pursue them to where they bed up in the dense thickets. Over the years, we discovered that 90 percent of our game kills were made before 9 a.m. At that rate, brunch might just as well be any time after 10 a.m. Anyone can wait that long, and by then they'll have worked up an appetite and everything tastes better, too. So there you are. For the mere price of this book you've just learned a pile of things that took me over 40 years to figure out. I hope that at least some of them will be as useful to you as they have been to me.

Now all you have to do is test for slack on the diamonds, tighten your cinches, and head for the high country.

TAMING EAST KOOTENAY RANCHERS AND ELK

Legendary stories, wild tales, horse lore, and hunting advice—they all come rolling out at the end of the day when your stomach's full, you've made your peace with the world, and you're sitting around warming your bones by the fire. But when the banter turns to more serious matters, there's one subject that always gets me fired up, and I expect it always will.

I don't know how it's been with you, but over the years, regardless of all the "la-di-da" cowboy and rancher stories that still circulate, I've had a few differences with the open-range cattle industry of B.C. There is a vast difference between ranchers who raise cattle and sheep on private property and those who rely on the "open range," or, to be more accurate with the phrasing, the public grasslands. As a matter of fact, there were times when life for all of us would have been a whole lot more pleasant if I'd never crossed paths with open-range ranchers. As it happened, though, fate won out, and depending on your point of view we did make life more interesting for one another.

The episode I'm about to relate is well recorded—by the ranchers of East Kootenay, by the region's Fish and Wildlife Branch (F&WB), by the RCMP, by the *Daily Townsman* newspaper in Cranbrook, by the various Rod and Gun clubs of the area, and by my own diaries of the winter I worked there.

This all goes back to the winter of 1975–76 when I got a contract with the F&WB to feed wild elk in the southern end of the East Kootenay. This is an area of southeastern B.C. that stretches between Skookumchuck, TaTa Creek, Kimberly, Cranbrook, and south from there to Wardner and Jaffray. I took the job because this was one of the few times in my life when things in the Gang Ranch country had cooled down to a point where I felt it was safe to leave home for a while. Safe enough, at least, that I was confident I would not return home to a pile of ashes. Money was a factor, although it was not the only reason. My decision to relocate temporarily also had to do with comments from several quarters—friends who said that they thought I was becoming too paranoid about my rancher neighbours here in the Chilcotin. One person even suggested I needed a break, that I should go out and live in more civilized society before I self-destructed. Right! But I went south anyway to give it a try.

Along with these personal factors there was another, more subtle, reason that I applied for this particular job. At that time there was a government proposal to re-introduce elk into the Chilcotin. If that were going to happen, the most likely spot for the first elk release was apparently right here in the Gang Ranch area. As I was the only permanent resident living close to the proposed release site, I would've been the most natural protector and recorder of the coming herd. (My nearest neighbours to this day are at the Sky Ranch, which is about ten saddle-horse miles away.)

The F&WB biologist of the day—and the major promoter of this scheme—was a man named Harold Mitchell. He'd gone out of his way to inform us that civilians were going to have to carry most of the responsibility for the elk and had urged us to begin organizing a protective screen for them. He was worried that some area ranchers were capable of doing something clandestine to stop the elk from arriving, or doing something to them after they had. It seemed we were of one mind on that point.

So the Guide Outfitters of B.C. and the B.C. Wildlife Federation formed a joint lobby group and began negotiating for the financial commitment and political support that were needed to ensure there would be no such hang-ups. After considering these circumstances, I felt that going to the East Kootenay would allow me to study control measures already in place there, measures that we might eventually have to implement in the Chilcotin.

Most ranchers in the Cariboo-Chilcotin were violently against having wild elk reintroduced here. They kept harping on that their alfalfa fields would receive the brunt of the damage should any of our plans go haywire. The pro-elk faction knew that such a risk was real, but we had also come to terms with using a fairly radical control measure. After some debate we'd agreed that with the arrival of the first elk, any truly nuisance animals should be shot. This tactic was not allowed in the East Kootenay.

We'd also proposed building elk-proof haystack enclosures in the problem areas, but the ranchers were still vetoing anything and everything to do with elk. And while the threat to private lands was the upfront argument the ranchers were using, I knew there was an underlying agenda that few would admit to, and that was their absolute opposition to having to share the public grasslands with wild grass-eaters once more.

By the mid-1970s there were few wild horses left in these parts and only the occasional sighting of an elk herd, a remnant of the kind of herds that had flourished here up to the time of Whitman's arrival. Aboriginal people were also well put down by then, pretty much penned up in their Canadian-style concentration camps. So the ranchers could truthfully claim that all of the Cariboo-Chilcotin was "cattle country." And as long as they could help it, there was no goddamned way they were going to allow any other grass-eaters to come along and be in competition with their cows.

Furthermore, a deep-seated cattleman attitude was prevalent in these parts. Many Interior ranchers at that time were ex-Americans—men who had been in the U.S. ranching business before they moved here. Since they'd already been through the "cattle vs. wildlife thing" down in the States, they brought stories with them that influenced their local ranching brethren. What they'd learned, they said, was that when the public gets involved in resource management they'll opt almost every time for wildlife—*especially* for elk. They warned every rancher around here that this "social disease" would spread like wildfire if it were ever able to get a start.

And since that was exactly the way we read it too, that was the reason we were so sure that our elk proposal would eventually take off and run. And why shouldn't it, after all? Whose grassland was it anyway?

In this part of B.C., elk are not an exotic species. By carbon dating several old elk horns, Harold Mitchell learned that elk have been around here for at least 1,000 years, so they're a damn sight more traditional than horses or cattle. Why did they die off? Nobody has been able to figure that out, although from carbon dating elk bones in various parts of the U.S., biologists have learned that elk numbers cycle from great highs to great lows. They still do not know why that is, but for those of us on the wild side of the issue, all the research made us feel we had a pretty good case for re-establishment. In the end, the main reason I went to the East Kootenay that winter was to try to learn something first-hand about controlling elk, especially problem elk.

My Orientation Begins

I had never been in the East Kootenay, and immediately after arriving I made contact with my new bosses at the F&WB: Ray Demarchi and Dave Phelps. Ray was the region's wildlife biologist and was considered by many to be an authority on Rocky Mountain elk; Dave was in charge of making plans and getting things done. He was my immediate boss, while Ray appeared to be the theory-and-idea man of the team. Last I heard, Dave Phelps was still working out of the Cranbrook office, but I cannot recall his title. It doesn't matter anyway, because the East Kootenay F&WB was not the type of outfit where people clicked their heels or saluted each other. As I was soon to learn, getting the job done was all that mattered, and in my opinion that's a pretty hard system to beat.

Ray Demarchi's credentials as an authority on elk were sometimes brought into question. Credibility depended a lot

The Demarchis come to visit. Here I am with Ray (left) and his son Don at Gaspard Lake. Birds of a feather always seem to flock together.

on who you were talking to: a rancher or a hunter. Ray considered himself a negotiator, someone whose duty was to represent the entire wildlife side when dealing with public resource planning and resolving the kind of resource conflicts that were then arising in the East Kootenay. In B.C. this was a new process. At the same time, in some parts of the district I heard ranchers suggest that he had considerable expertise in creating the conflicts, too. This perspective could hardly be doubted when you considered that Ray was seen as the person most responsible for resurrecting the local elk population from a diminishing herd into an alarmingly expanding one. It all boiled down to the fact that he was trying to protect wildlife from a still new, and expanding, agriculture industry—an industry that was usurping natural forage from almost all wildlife, especially elk.

Most of these clashes were not new ground to me, as we had been through a lot of similar conflict in the Chilcotin. The difference was that the Chilcotin had been settled and overwhelmed by cattlemen interests a hundred years earlier.

For some reason, the East Kootenay was still going through the growing pains (or dying pains, depending on your point of view), so for me it was like watching a rerun. Still, this was not the Chilcotin of the 1870s or the Gang Ranch country of the present day. Apparently a more modern drama was going to unfold in much more civilized ways. (Oh sure!)

Against this backdrop it had been arranged that I was to go back to school again, and my teachers had volunteered to run me through the grades. I must say they were pretty darn good at it too. Ray, in particular, had a forceful personality, and it didn't take long for the pupil to realize that he should pay attention because Ray's observations and theories seemed to be more often right than wrong. Sometimes I would wake up at night laughing at the day-and-night difference between my 1976 instructors and the teachers I'd had 35 years earlier, who'd been about as interesting as train whistles. Or perhaps it was the difference in subject matter that had an awakening effect on me. Who knows?

When I arrived in the East Kootenay that winter I set up my work base at the old Kimberly Airport at TaTa Creek, a place that had recently been turned into an F&WB research station. Three other biologists were also working on wildlife projects there: Brian Churchill, who was accompanied by his wife; Bob Jamieson, who was "batching" like me; and Chris and Shelly Smith with their two small kids. We each had our own house, and I was not completely alone in mine as I had brought along my hunting and trail partner, who by then was pretty much a one-man dog. Shep was always good company, totally obedient, and he enjoyed new trails, smells, and experiences as much as I did.

The domestic arrangements settled, it did not take me long to realize that even though the Kootenay region was similar to the Cariboo-Chilcotin, there were also some interesting contrasts. The first thing that caught my attention was that there didn't seem to be much in the way of what I'd learned to consider true grassland. From Ray's earlier stories I'd been under the impression that the East Kootenay wildlife vs. cattle problem had stemmed from grass, but from what I could see, there wasn't

The old control tower at the Kimberly Airport, which was turned into a research lab for Fish and Wildlife Branch (F&WB).

enough of the stuff there to argue about. Even though the government and the provincial cattle industry were touting the region as open-range country suitable for commercial cattle raising, a person didn't need a degree in agriculture to begin questioning that classification.

Simply put, it's not good cow country, at least not when compared with the Okanagan, Nicola, Cariboo, or Chilcotin. All the same, a couple of days spent driving the back roads—and there are many that follow the little creeks that come tumbling down out of the Rocky and Purcell Mountains—turned up clusters of recently constructed buildings and fences on almost every flat spot. Most gates had signs informing the passing traveller that these were, indeed, cattle ranches.

With the exception of a very few, however, they could much more accurately be described as hobby farms or "ranchettes." Their limited size was the most obvious difference from the ranches farther west. The similarities were most notable in the magical effect of agricultural subsidies, which can transform baseline reality into something else altogether. I do not mean that in a positive way, either—unless you happen to be the owner of a subsidized ranch.

I've always marvelled at the amazing ability some have to force beef out of rocks, because it's obvious that there cannot be any "bottom line" economics in that type of ranching or farming. But somehow beef does manage to grow out of rockpiles, and it makes a person wonder about the true cost, about who is paying and what the hell for. I have heard agricultural apologists claim that there is a social benefit to keeping people on these marginal farms, but that still doesn't account for the most obvious sub-marginal operations. Where are the benefits from those? Having a green mind, I say we should let these follies slide back into a wilderness that has always held the world in a state of fallow, which I've found to be a pretty nice state to live in. Without question, green is a better condition than the brownouts of artificial economics and values.

Feeding and Foraging

So much for that; sermon's over. After a couple of days getting oriented and settling into my new digs at the airport, I checked in with the main F&WB office in Cranbrook where Ray, Dave, and I plotted out my winter work schedule. The job I'd undertaken involved feeding alfalfa hay to six different elk herds that descended from the Rocky and Purcell Mountains to winter in the main valley along the Kootenay River. There were two reasons why the F&WB was artificially feeding these elk: one was to draw them away from ranchers' haystacks; the other was to relieve pressure on the remaining elk wintering grounds, natural areas that had not yet been usurped by the ranching industry.

A serious forage problem had been created—and was still evolving—as a result of all the small ranches that had been allowed to develop along the traditional wildlife winter ranges in those creek valleys. Wild animals, elk in particular, are persistent in their use of traditional ranges and travel corridors. Now that the ranchers had homesteaded the established elk range, most elk affected refused to relocate. And that was only part of the problem. Even if the elk had wanted to move, the crunch came when you confronted the reality that there were few other places for them to winter. There never has been any surplus range or forage in the East Kootenay. So the F&WB vs. rancher arguments centred around one simple question: were elk compounding the cattle problem or could it be vice versa?

This question came to the fore every year along about Christmastime, when the ranchers would wake up one frosty morning and look out to discover several hundred wild visitors had returned to their "former" wintering grounds. Often the elk would have moved right into the stack yards of alfalfa hay, just like they had it figured that ranchers, in their benevolent way, had piled all that fine feed there for their benefit. Once an elk gets a taste of good alfalfa, the habit is as hard to break as a skid row bum's welfare handout.

Twenty years earlier there'd been more open grassland in the lower part of the Kootenay River, but the previous provincial government had been in cahoots with the Yanks, letting them use the Canadian side as a water storage area for their Libby Dam project. This had the effect of tumbling all "lesser" problems back on top of one another, and it was all working out the way Ray Demarchi had predicted. There were still enough smaller wild grasslands above the high-water line to support the elk if they could move up into them. But when other branches of government—such as the Department of Agriculture and the B.C. Forest Service—decided to use their end of the lopsided resource table to commandeer that grass for the ranching industry, the elk were once again left out in the cold.

By the time I arrived in the East Kootenay the sparks were flying over the forage conflict. The issue was already at such a heated pitch that you were well advised to study your table company carefully before being drawn into a discussion in a bar. The topic was so hot it could draw the colour out of ranchers' faces and put a flinty look in their eyes. At the same time, nobody was denying the fact that the grasslands were deteriorating from overgrazing by both wild and domestic ungulates. That was why the F&WB was developing the artificial feeding program that I was to work on.

The ranchers of the East Kootenay came to hate the sight of this truck so much, and made their opinions known politically, that Ray Demarchi had me tape over my name, which was painted on the truck doors. Of course by the time it was done, it was a bit late, as every rancher in the area knew who and what the brown truck represented. And so it went.

The scene at a feeding site. Very few bulls come when the truck is there. Instead, they feed at night.

The program was not scheduled to go on forever only until the range improved to the point where the feeding would no longer be required. Since nobody could be certain how long that might take, there was a lot of guesswork involved, and the project could best be described as very experimental. From the F&WB side of the forage allotment, Ray was hoping to get the ranchers to agree that wildlife did, in fact, have a legal right to a share of the grass. And while there were a few ranchers in the area who were willing to concede that point, there were others who were nowhere near agreeing to such heresy.

The Subtleties of Subsidies

When I arrived, the elk-feeding program was into its second year, and there were still many unanswered questions as to its long-term value. About the only thing that was keeping it afloat was public awareness all across B.C. of the whys and wherefores of the forage problem, to the extent that politicians were fearful of curtailing it. I believe the major reason the opposition was lying low was because of keen public interest. Elk are very visible when herded up on their wintering areas, and people were travelling long distances to come and view the spectacle along the narrow Columbia Valley. This, in turn, was making the ranchers nervous.

What we all noticed—even the more enlightened ranchers—was that the public seemed to look more favourably upon elk than the ranching industry, and they wanted their 20,000 elk to be given fair, perhaps even preferential, treatment over cows. From conversations in the bars at night, though, I determined that any mention of this within hearing of most of the ranchers I met was still considered anathema. Efforts to encourage them to shift their thinking were about as popular as trying to sell euthanasia to a Catholic Church congregation.

Back at the old Kimberly Airport, all my neighbours had been briefing me on the history of the Kootenay cattle and wildlife situation, and one of their points is still clear in my mind. It was this: prior to 1956 there were few cattle ranches in the East Kootenay. This seemed odd, because Whitman had settled the

Whitetail deer come to the elk feeding area as well.

area long before that. Perhaps it was a case of the old-timers being wise enough to realize that the area was not well suited for raising cattle, so the real cattlemen bypassed it for greener pastures elsewhere. Now it was being settled by a somewhat more desperate type of greenhorn, who figured he could force beef out of a rockpile. To back this theory up, only a short while later, by the 1960s, agricultural subsidy programs had increased to such a degree that economic realities could be staved off almost indefinitely. (At least so long as the pork barrel was kept supplied.) One of the F&WB whiz-kid informants mentioned that he had done a fast calculation on the agricultural subsidy programs of that time and had arrived at the theory that Canada was going into debt at the rate of about $2 billion a year to keep unprofitable farms and ranches from reverting back to the grasslands these homesteaders should never have been allowed to plough under in the first place. The finding was very interesting.

Apparently this enterprising researcher was not alone in his line of thinking. By the 1970s, a lot of East Kootenay folk had begun to raise some serious questions about the wisdom of taxpayers supporting an artificial beef industry. The reason the questions arose here first was because many of the local people had deliberately moved to the region because of its world-famous diversified wildlife herds.

That little item had been well recorded all the way back to the middle of the nineteenth century and was a catalyst for organizing some of the most active and aggressive Rod and Gun clubs that B.C. has ever seen. In the mid-1970s, when I was there, their members far outnumbered the East Kootenay ranchers. It seemed the only way the ranchers were managing to hold on to the land and outside resources was through connections with and endorsements from the ranching industry in other parts of North America, places where the art of political lobbying had been learned. It worked out something like this: anybody who owned more than 50 cows qualified to call himself a rancher and automatically became one of the "Good ol' Boys." Another of my East Kootenay informants lumped the entire theory into one sentence that, for me, says it all. "The ranching industry of North America learned a long time ago how to take the politicians out to lunch."

By coupling these theories with my previous experiences in the Cariboo and Chilcotin areas it was easy to conclude that all my earlier suspicions were correct. Any type of business that can succeed in hiding behind the facade of the word "agriculture" is still politically sacred, because even though farmer votes are expensive, they are simple to buy.

Spiker

So there I was driving 180 miles a day, collecting a salary plus mileage on my 4x4 truck as I loaded, hauled, and scattered hay around to elk at six different feeding sites. That may not sound like a lot of work, but those roads early in the morning were often goddamn slippery. Even with a 4x4 that had a ton of hay on it, I'd wind up doing doughnuts on the paved roads. After I got off the pavement, I often had to chain the truck to get up into some of the rougher feeding grounds. The scattering of hay took time. Feeding elk is nothing like feeding domestic livestock because the elk tend to be great squabblers and like to feed alone or, at most, in small family gatherings. So the hay has to be scattered accordingly.

It takes three loads like this each day, and a 180-mile round trip, to feed the elk.

Elk are great squabblers on a feeding ground, so the feed must be scattered more widely than with domestic animals or the elk will spend too much energy chasing each other away rather than actually feeding themselves.

As all of the East Kootenay was strange country to me, Dave Phelps came along on the first day to show me where and how he wanted the feed laid out. One of the places that Dave guided me to was named Frenchman's Slough, and the actual feed site was located up on a hill in old logging slash. A small ranch and the remnants of the town of Wardner were nearby. The plan at this location was to draw the elk away from the adjacent rancher's haystacks. According to Dave, the fellow was not well disposed towards elk and objected to them being anywhere on his property.

Dave and I drove up into the feeding ground and scattered hay around; there were not many elk tracks to indicate that the herd had moved down from the mountains yet. We were just about to drive away when we noticed the truck had a flat tire. Normally that wouldn't have been a big deal, but we had to dig the spare out from under a ton of hay before changing it onto the truck.

No sooner were we moving again and heading down the main road when, as I was about to gear up a notch, I noticed the truck was acting sluggish. I pulled over to the side of the road to check things out and, lo and behold, what did we have but another flat tire! That first flat was annoying, but this second one was a real disaster. How many spares do most people carry on their pickups? Well, that's exactly how many I carried too.

So with the better part of a ton of hay still on the truck and no sign of traffic on this country road, we knew that we would be walking until we located some assistance. Since it was closer than going to Wardner, Dave reckoned our best bet was to walk to the ranch. Dave also figured that even though the rancher did not like elk, he would be friendly enough to either lend us a spare or let us use his phone to call someone at the F&WB to come to our rescue. While all this was under consideration, there was a buzzing suspicion growing in the back of my mind about the condition of the side road we'd just turned off. I suggested to Dave that we go check it out first, before it snowed again, because there was no question that something had just flattened two almost-new tires.

We didn't have to walk far back up the road before we found the problem. Only it was not one problem we discovered but ten! Someone had carefully embedded ten railroad spikes into the muddy ruts of the road before everything had frozen over a few days before. We could tell that it had been done recently, as the saboteur had used small, brushy tree limbs to camouflage each spike. The trap had been well planned, too, and could only have been set by someone who was acquainted with the area and who knew a lot about elk movements to and from that feeding ground (which had also been used the previous year). Whoever the culprit was had the entire scenario plotted out, and that made us wonder just who hated elk so much that they would go to this extreme.

I didn't know a soul within 400 miles, but Dave knew everybody around there and he had his suspicions. He kept telling me that nothing like this had ever happened before. He seemed to be in a state of shock now that it had happened and that, as a result, we were going to have to find a way to deal with it.

Well Dave may have been shocked, but I knew I was still in rancher country, so the situation didn't surprise me all that much. The more I thought about it, the more I felt like I was back home in the Chilcotin. In the Gang Ranch country I'd already met with "mysterious" road spikes; they had become one of those things you have to take in your stride. Back home, though, we always knew the identity of the outfit that encouraged such tactics, and once in a while we even figured out who was actually responsible for the deeds. I'd had two contingency plans for handling such circumstances: one was to get in the habit of carrying at least two spare tires; the other was to begin squeezing the outfit responsible until it made its people back off. Sometimes that even worked.

That day in Coal Valley made me realize that the East Kootenay was not home to me yet, and being there among strangers meant it was going to be a new ball game altogether. It was obvious that life was not going to be dull.

We pulled up a few spikes and left the others in place as evidence. Dave said he would be bringing the RCMP into the matter as he felt it had more authority than the F&WB to control acts like this. He said he didn't want the situation to escalate any further, and I noticed he made deliberate eye contact with me as he emphasized this point. Well that only made sense because, as we both agreed, ownership of booby-traps is hard to prove unless the police can squeeze a confession out of somebody. And by 1975 they were not supposed to be doing things like that anymore.

Right at that moment, though, we had no alternative but to resume walking, and we ended up having to trudge three miles to the nearest ranch. I remember that Dave had a bad cold that day, and as our nature walk progressed and we discussed our predicament, he grew more and more angry. When we finally got to the ranch, the owner was home all right. But when Dave told him why we were there and asked if we could use his phone, the old bastard kept us out on the porch for several minutes while he hemmed and hawed and belly-ached about there being too goddamned many elk in the country. The diatribe had me wondering if we were going to be walking all the way to Wardner after all, until he finally relented and let Dave go in to use the phone. In many ways I found their conversation enlightening, and it had the effect of putting a lot of my recent grey areas into absolutely clear perspective.

When Dave finished making the arrangements for a mounted tire to be brought out to us, the rancher pretty much bum-rushed us out of his house and off his property, which I thought was hilarious. This was the same rancher that Dave had described an hour earlier as "a bit eccentric, but not really a bad fellow." Right!

Walking back to the truck we resumed our discussion about our situation and the greeting we'd received at the ranch, which was upsetting Dave no end. While agreeing with him, the other side of me did sort of admire the old bastard's gall, because Dave was a government official, a game warden or some such thing. And he probably had some legal authority, perhaps like a forest ranger. So for this fellow to practically tell Dave to shove off took some jam. I know that I have my quirks, but when people in distress come to my door, even government officials, I've never had the nerve to treat them the way that rancher treated Dave. Hell, I've even helped ranchers out of mud holes, never mind granting a small favour such as using the phone. It takes a certain type of personality to behave the way that rancher did.

Our wheel eventually arrived and we were able to continue on our way. Later that day the RCMP went out to Frenchman's Slough and pulled up the rest of the spikes, and for the next several days they conducted some sort of a quiet investigation. I was not directly involved as my bosses were representing me, but Dave Phelps kept me informed on the case.

Mostly, what they all seemed to be trying to establish was not so much the "who," but more the "why" of the matter. Dave and Ray met with the officers of the local Cattlemen's Association, and between them they figured they had cooled the spiker down. (By that time we all knew who it was, and nobody was challenging the assumption.) I don't remember whether the RCMP had a direct talk with the spiker, but everybody in the district knew the police were involved in the case. Most sideliners believed that in itself was enough to deter the spiker from striking again. I do remember the legal consequences that were debated, though. If we'd made it out onto the highway and our sabotaged tire had been responsible for somebody getting hurt, most people thought charges would automatically have been in the second degree—and that could have meant a government vacation of more than ten years.

Smoking out the Culprit

Even though it was obvious the attack had been aimed at the elk, I was the one most affected, and it made me more than a little angry watching the situation being so quietly taken care of in this way. I decided to smoke the culprit out, using my old standby of writing a letter to the editor of a newspaper. I knew that many Rod and Gunners in the district had been deeply involved in setting up the elk-feeding program, so rather than write a letter to the larger provincial papers, I addressed it to the local *Townsman*, a daily newspaper published in Cranbrook.

The letter was a typical Choate concoction, phrased in such a way that it would cause the most sparks to fly. I mentioned the "velvet glove" handling of the spiker, which I felt (and still feel) deferred too much to the cattle industry and protected people who like to be portrayed as "pillars of society"—a perception they have spent 200 years in North America trying to cultivate. A great many people have been snowed by that approach, but there are still a few of us who have not. Do you believe in social privilege? Well I don't either, and if ever there was a made-to-order opportunity to point out to the general public that it is, nevertheless, alive and flourishing in Canada, this had to be it.

I made all kinds of comparisons, asking whether readers believed the incident would have been quietly hushed up if it had been an ambulance, a police car, or a fire truck damaged in this way. So why one and not the other, especially when the vehicle in question was also being used in public service? I still have a copy of that letter around here some place, but by now you should have a pretty good gist of what was in it. What this letter had going for it, above all else, was that it was based on absolute fact. If anybody tried to challenge it, it would simply pave the way for more information to come to light. Without consulting anybody else, I sealed the envelope and mailed it.

Within a couple of days the letter began to produce results, one of which was a message from my bosses to come into Cranbrook and appear at a meeting to discuss it. That was no problem because I'd anticipated it and, furthermore, I was being paid to go to the meeting, which I believe was both a first and a last for me. Upon arrival, I was surprised to learn that the *Townsman* had not yet published the letter, but had taken it to the F&WB for verification. Along with a lot of other people I'd never met, a rep from the newspaper was in attendance at the meeting. In addition, there were at least two reps from the local sportsmen associations, some officers from the Cattlemen's Association, personnel from both the F&WB and the B.C. Forest Service, and I believe at least one of the fellows in civvies (who was never introduced) was probably RCMP. So there were going to be sparks after all! It seemed the only person who was *not* there was the spiker.

My first impression as I scanned the gathering was that the cattlemen were acting extremely nervous, and some of the government folks could hardly be said to be at ease. I suspected that had something to do with the presence of the official public witnesses—the reporter and the sportsmen sitting there flapping their ears. The ranchers also had a right to be nervous. It was common knowledge that many East Kootenay sportsmen held little love for the ranching industry, and the information that would be coming out of this meeting, they must have thought, could possibly have far-reaching consequences, maybe even incite a sabotage war between ranchers and sportsmen.

Well that was exactly the way I viewed the possibilities, and I figured it might be a damn good thing if that happened. There's nothing like a hot little war to make people realize they should find other ways to resolve their differences. The seriousness of the situation had a sobering effect on most of the people there that day.

After we'd all had our say, the final decision was left up to me. The *Townsman* seemed prepared to go ahead and publish the letter. After all, why not? Not one person had offered a denial nor even questioned the reasoning behind why it had happened. In a small town and rural district, how often do things like this happen, especially when there is the strong possibility that the culprit could not only be charged, but be convicted too? Aren't actions like this supposed to be redressed by the legal notion we call *justice*?

Everyone was waiting for my reply to a question from whoever was chairing the meeting, asking whether I would consider withdrawing the letter. For somebody like me, that was a question to ponder, and my situation was soon brought into clearer light. A fellow from either the F&WB or the Forest Service, sitting beside and a little behind me, leaned forward and quietly reminded me of something I'd never had to deal with before.

"Chilco," he said, "in situations like this you are expected to remember, at least for the time being, that you are one of us now and not the wild, loose cannon you're used to being." I'm sure everybody in the room heard him and I knew that he was sort of right. But still, it was spinning through my mind that I've always had little faith in negotiators and better-than-par luck on a battlefield, which has always been my preference. This time I wavered too long, finally conceding to what was being a little-less-than-subtly suggested and withdrawing the letter. Even now—perhaps especially now—with the hindsight of 25 years' reflection, I believe that for the long term I made the wrong choice. Because I still see that goddamn privilege overriding too many resource-use decisions. Not only that, but the goddamn spiker cost me $300—after a tire shop inspected my tires, I discovered all four were damaged.

Push Comes to Shove

Are all ranchers the same or is it just me who's paranoid? I really began wondering about that a few days after the spiking episode. This time I was feeding elk at another site near Skookumchuck, which is about 50 miles from Frenchman's Slough, when I crossed paths and viewpoints with another rancher. I'd just finished the feeding and driven out onto the main road when a pickup truck cut me off and came to a halt right in front of me. The driver, an obvious rancher-type, came striding back to my truck and shouted through the window, "What the hell were you doing over in that field?" Sitting in my truck I explained that I was working for the F&WB and that I'd just laid out an elk-feeding site on the far side of that "government-owned" field. Well now, did he ever explode! He began cursing the elk, the F&WB, the goddamn hunters, and probably a few others I have now forgotten about. One hundred pounds heavier, I thought, and he would have been a dead ringer for the manager of the Gang Ranch.

After he'd run out of steam a bit he must have thought he was in full control of the situation, because that was when he advised me in belligerent tones that I'd better not show up there with feed for the elk again. This being the end of a ten-hour day, I was tired both physically and mentally, and that statement came across as a little more than I was prepared to take. In a flash I arrived at the conclusion that I didn't like anything about this loud-mouthed bastard. He obviously knew who and what I was, but all I knew about him was what could be gained from his appearance and attitude, and that pretty much told me all I needed to know. Which was that we'd just gone past the amount of East Kootenay rancher shit that I was going to take.

As I said earlier, my bosses and neighbours had advised me that the Kootenay country was well settled into civilized manners. Accordingly, I wasn't carrying an equalizer in the truck. A quick once-over of this guy told me he and I were about the same size and that he didn't appear to be armed either. So as everything mentally came together in an instant, I concluded that this quiet country road was as good a place as any to settle a few opinions and accounts.

I opened the door of the truck and swung out, both feet hitting the ground together, then started for the son of a bitch. It quickly appeared this was not exactly how he wanted the discussion to proceed, because he cooled off faster than you can imagine, backed up to his own truck, hopped in, and closed the door behind him. I forget whether he locked it or not, and I never tried opening it. Instead, we continued our talk through his window rather than mine, and after a few more lippy opinions from him about elk, he finally drove away.

Living under the shadow of adversity most of my life, it seemed I'd learned to thrive on it. Several of my friends even mentioned this trait. Now, however, I suddenly remembered what had been said at the recent letter meeting, the suggestions about how I was supposed to conduct myself. So I decided it might be wise for me to share this experience with my boss, to see if he had any better ideas on how to resolve these kinds of disagreements other than by force.

Later that evening I phoned Dave Phelps at his home because I wanted some official answers before I went out on the job again the following morning. During the phone conversation, I told him that for my own safety I was going to start packing an equalizer, just in case. From Dave I discovered (or rediscovered) that neither he nor government agencies in general take well to the idea of direct action. So he asked me to simply stay away from that particular feed site for a few days while he poured oil on the waves.

And that's what I did, even though I neglected to tell any of my bosses that for about the next month there was an equalizer in my truck. Perhaps Dave's way was the right way, because about two days after the confrontation he sent me word to reopen the feed site, and that was the last time the East Kootenay ranchers and I ever locked horns.

It was, and still is, hard to say why they backed off then, but I suspected that one of the reasons might have been because word had gotten around the district, especially among the hunting fraternity. I was brought up to date on that notion a short time later when I stopped in for a beer at the pub in Wasa. A table of obvious hunter-types invited me over and informed me that some of them were circulating word to the ranchers, saying if they didn't back off they were going to discover that their cattle were just as vulnerable as elk. Now here were people I knew how to relate to!

Lessons in Land Use

I'd gone to the Kootenay country to learn about elk, but my teachers also gave me lessons on other land- and resource-use issues that were then being negotiated in that area. The negotiations were being done through a new allocation system called Coordinated Resource Management Plans (CRMP), which in B.C. was an emerging method of resource-use planning. In the past there had been little public input into such things. Most resource- and land-use plans had been decided and handed down by government bureaucracies. By the 1970s, though, many of these decisions were being viewed by a growing number of people as "top down" results. Too often there were strange little coincidences that smacked of favouritism, and it was all beginning to jell into a groundswell of public suspicion about who government bureaucrats might really be serving.

So the powers that be decided to give this new planning system a try and began the experiment in the Kootenay country.

This was not surprising as Dave and Ray were the major instigators for importing the system to B.C. from the United States, where most of the theories and principles behind CRMP had originated. Like others before them who introduced a new "rock-the-boat" system, they both lost and gained friends for their efforts.

In these matters, the first priority always has to be establishing the size of the pie, agreeing to what it's made of, and going from there. In my experience, every single one of these meetings seems to be managed by the B.C. Forest Service. Its reps lead off by trying to establish the theory that every tree is theirs to grind up into boards or chips. They continue by reinforcing the idea that every blade of forage is theirs to turn into beef or mutton. Finally, they conclude by arguing that if anything whatsoever is to be preserved in an ongoing natural state for use by wildlife or recreationists, it will be done only at their discretion. The Forest Service reps are immediately followed by the timber companies and the ranchers, who simply reiterate that the Forest Service view is the way it's going to be—as if they were here first and had established prior rights.

The first thing I noticed about so-called public planning is that the table is nowhere near to being round, all due to the devious ways of politics. A natural selection process keeps it that way. The commercial users have financial interests to protect, but the wildlife preservationists, recreationists, and whoever else volunteers to be there have no financial incentive. Even if there is a vague material reward motivating some of them, it's nowhere near what's at stake for commercial forest users. To make the system even more skewed, there seems to be a kind of collusion between industry and government to stretch these plans out into an almost endless number of meetings—meetings the general public is not being paid to go to and cannot afford to attend repeatedly in order to stay on top of the never-ending process. When industry and government begin to see their personal objectives becoming overpowered, they simply revert to starving out the opposition by piling on more meetings.

I can tell you truthfully that I've *never* seen even one of these meetings chaired by an impartial person. None of us should ever allow ourselves to be conned into believing that government employees are allowed to be impartial, because their political paymasters will not allow it, especially when it comes to resource-use decisions.

If you don't believe that, take a look at how these decisions have turned out. I've never yet attended a so-called public-input meeting where the first question from the chair was "Is there a consensus to use this area commercially?" Instead, every one of these meetings opens in reverse, with government telling us that the area has already been committed to commercial use, even to the point of explaining how many units of wood are going to come from it, or how many cows it's going to accommodate. Then they entrust the meeting with putting together a plan to accommodate all their preordained political commitments. Democracy can have a very flexible meaning. If ever there is to be a binding referendum, there is no issue more deserving of a province-wide vote than resource use. But will any political party ever allow that to happen?

In the East Kootenay of the early-to-mid 1970s the CRMP system did get off to a pretty good start, mostly, I suspect, because the bureaucrats, politicians, and industry people hadn't caught on to what could happen when the plans were implemented. The main reason the process got going in the region was without doubt because of elk, or to be more accurate, the problem elk (also known as nuisance elk and sour elk depending on who is describing them).

Returning each year to their old wintering grounds, these elk caused havoc when they broke down ranchers' fences, but that turned out to be the easiest problem to solve. The F&WB, usually with cooperation from the affected rancher, simply went into the bush and mapped out the traditional elk trails where they crossed these new fences. Together, they rebuilt several panels of fence at these spots so the fence could be easily laid down each fall after the cows came home, and then raised again in the spring after the elk migrated back up the mountain. As an old ranch-hand from moose country, I could see that this system had a lot of merit, because it's a hell of a lot easier to open and close a special section of fence than it is to repair one that's been torn open by any kind of animal.

The next elk problem was also easily solved—all it took was better protection for haystacks. To begin with, most ranchers had built simple wire fences to keep their own horses and cattle out. But a few ranchers had been wise enough to use slab lumber cut into eight- or ten-foot lengths, wiring them up on end to the original horizontal fence. For the three months I lived in the Kootenay that winter, I never saw any sign that an elk had managed to jump over this kind of fence. I was impressed enough with the system that I took several pictures, and after I returned home I built modified versions—cutting small pine poles and using them instead of mill slabs. No moose or horse has ever gotten through them to steal hay here, either.

Down in the Kootenay, Dave Phelps and Ray Demarchi were encouraging the local hunting clubs to help ranchers with the modifications, and some government money was invested as well. So there was beginning to be a bit of cooperation in all the coordination and planning. What's more, the simple solutions were working.

Another elk problem the ranchers wanted something done about at that time had to do with what they called "homesteader" elk. Rather than climbing up and down the mountains all summer, searching for what was usually a lesser quality wild forage, these elk develop a taste for young alfalfa plants in new hay fields. You can hardly blame them—up until the 1950s it was their range to use as they pleased. Now man had come along and seeded those areas with the richest forage plants known to exist, and elk are known to be fast learners when something seems important to them. And what is more important to any creature than food?

In the mid-1970s those homesteader elk were still a big stumbling block to cooperation. To alleviate this problem, the plan was to begin rotating the cattle range so the high-quality natural feed might encourage the elk to stay away from the new-sown fields. The practice of rotating livestock ranges was well known in most of the rest of the world, but in B.C. it had hardly ever been done. Most established ranchers want little or nothing to do with it because it usually boils downs to fewer cattle or sheep on the range.

The equation is easy to understand. Most established ranchers had long ago set their own terms for using the range, and in most cases, naturally, foraging was maximized. So if ranchers were ordered to use only half or a third of the range in any given year, there was no way the smaller pieces of land would support their existing herds for a full season. Hence, fewer livestock, etc. The truth is—and everybody with an ounce of sense knows this and always has—rotation is something that the livestock industry should have adopted from the beginning. Why it was ignored when these 1950-vintage ranches started up I've never heard, but I suspect bad politics and corrupt bureaucrats were to blame.

According to my East Kootenay teachers, they had trouble getting some of the ranchers involved with the CRMP process until they began to realize that rotation might become the official policy for resource use. If ranchers never came to the table, their neighbours might conveniently cut themselves some good deals at the absentees' expense. So it might be better to go and get something, they reasoned, than stay at home and perhaps get less or even nothing. There is a word in the English language for this incentive system, and when non-government people use it it's called "blackmail." Think what you like, it does seem to work.

There were a lot of other things being discussed at those CRMP tables of the 1970s, but by now you must be getting a fairly good picture of what was beginning to happen. For those of us on the wild side, the situation appeared to be more positive than before because, like it or not, industry was having to recognize wildlife as legitimate users of the land, something that had been rare in the past.

Elk Adaptation

The rest of that winter was politically uneventful, other than the everyday fact of living in new country and finally meeting some of the more "civilized" people that Ray Demarchi had promised populated the area. I managed to become totally immersed in what I'd gone there for—the herds of elk and other wildlife for which the East Kootenay has always been famous. The elk were impossible to ignore. They were literally everywhere, even feeding and bedding in the old flower garden under the front window of the house I was staying in.

They were so numerous that they could always be counted on in an emergency. For example, surprise encounters with elk were apparently a major cause of car wrecks on rural roads. (What ditched driver have you ever met who would admit to driving with what police refer to as undue care and attention?) All joking aside, though, there were many drivers who—going too fast to stop within 30 feet—ended up with an elk in their laps. I witnessed a sickening number of injured elk and crunched vehicles during my early morning feeding trips, arriving on the scene before the F&WB hauled the crippled elk away or the wreckers arrived to clear away the rest. Those elk taught me many things, the most striking characteristic being that they are without doubt the most adaptable animals I've ever come across.

They are opportunistic, too. When I met them on feed sites I quickly learned that they could be as sneaky as whitetail deer, and I was amazed to see how fast they figured out what side of the truck I worked from. Then they would rush up to the opposite side, grab a mouthful of hay, and run off to nonchalantly munch it down. As soon as one had done this a few times within sight of the more nervous types, it was only a matter of minutes before there was a whole stampede of them scrambling for their turn at the hay. Their behaviour can best be described as "hit and run," because an elk is fast. What's more, they are every bit as possessive of their place in the herd's pecking order as horses are, and this trait was just as strong among the cows and yearlings. They were the ones who most often came to the feed sites. The bulls, even the young ones, were more nervous than the females.

A few spike bulls fed with the cows, but by the time they had their second set of antlers they began behaving accordingly.

All the same, the pecking order was always being challenged, and sometimes, just to test them out, I would deliberately toss hay off the wrong side of the truck (or at least the opposite side to what they were expecting). When that happened a battle royal would ensue among the older cows to re-establish themselves on new ground. The cows were far more prone to fighting over things like that than the bulls, and I never did see a bull seriously challenge another over feed. But those older cows, *wow*! Did they ever make the fur fly sometimes.

Before that winter was over I developed some favourites at each feed site, and they knew it. I'm sure that in a little time I could have had some of them feeding out of my hands. But these animals were not protected in a park setting, and we did not want them to become too friendly, as that would have set them up for almost certain slaughter the next hunting season.

Also, it is well known that partially tame wild animals can be extremely dangerous to humans. They can become possessive and demanding of attention and if it does not come when they want it, they come for it anyway. All the same, when I was on the feed grounds with them, I always talked to the tamer ones. Before the winter was over, many of them had learned to talk back to me, mostly through eye and facial expressions, but sometimes with low coughs and snorts, not much different than conversations you'd have with a dog or horse. As a matter of fact, almost every animal species I've ever taken the time to test has responded to a sort of monotone human voice, almost like they're hypnotized by it. At least the ones that will stand close enough to hear.

I have gone into corrals full of mightily riled horses and, before trying to work with them, have just wandered among them talking quietly with that steady monotone voice. After a couple of hours of that, many of them will be standing there with a simple, drowsy expression. Don't get me wrong, though, because as soon as you try to take advantage of their stupor by touching them with a rope, they come back to their former state of alertness faster than you can imagine. This is the moment when many a horse wrangler has his head or ribs caved in. On the other hand, if time allows the wrangler to use this system several times on the same horse while not doing anything harmful, most can be brought a long way toward domesticity by such gentle persuasion. Remember that it takes time and patience—every horse or animal has its own limit as to how far it will allow itself to be conned by humans.

In the case of these feed-yard elk, it did not take them long to recognize the particular sound of my truck. When, in their estimation, I was late arriving at the sites, many would come trooping down to the main road and then jubilantly escort me back into the bush. Sometimes they would walk along so close to the truck that it was possible to reach out and touch them. I tried it once, but the immediate reaction taught me not to make a habit of it. A friendly old cow lashed out with a hind foot and put a hundred-dollar dent in the door of the truck, then jumped in front of it and stood there with the most indignant expression on her face you can imagine. Luckily the truck was going only five miles per hour, so other than the door thump, it was all harmless education.

I tried to further relations while on the feed grounds, but they were not receptive to familiarity there either. It reminded me of comparable situations between human beings. For instance, have you ever noticed the look a woman will give you for trying to run a hand over a restricted area before she is ready? Well, cow elk react exactly the same way, but for a lot more reasons. It seemed that human touch was an absolute no-no.

Hoodwinked

The whole subject of elk behaviour reminds me of another little incident from that winter that involved my dog, Shep. He used to travel everywhere in the cab of the truck with me. This was in the early part of the winter because before then Shep had never seen an elk at close quarters. His entire life had been spent around large animals, domestic and wild. Even though he was obedient about not chasing them until he was told he could, he still projected enough of a threat to ensure they kept at a respectful distance. He was no namby-pamby dog: I knew for sure he'd killed at least two coyotes, chased many moose and bears out of his yard, and he was well trained for following blood trails down to snarling climaxes. There was no question in my mind that Shep considered himself to be the meanest son of a bitch in any part of any country.

Not only was he very capable in those respects, but he also had a deep bark that could scare the shit out of any white-faced cow on the range, not to mention most people as well. He fully understood that he had this powerful ability to bluff, and there was nothing else in this world that pleased him more than to sit in his truck and clear the roads for us. He was better than any vehicle horn that's ever been invented. Yes, all was certainly well with the world when it came to Shep's experiences with animals in the Chilcotin.

His first introduction to close-range Kootenay elk, though, turned out to be nothing at all like he expected. It didn't turn out to be anything like I expected either. I'd driven out onto the feed yard where the elk, getting tamer by the day, didn't run from the truck, but just stood off to the side. It was obvious that they could see Shep sitting up on the seat beside me, and they were paying far more attention to him than they were to me. Although they were making no move to run, they most certainly were in a high state of alertness. So was Shep. As this was to be his first close encounter with these strange animals, I was extremely curious to see how he would react.

To begin with, he just stood on the seat with his tail and ruff puffed up, not saying a word, while his eyes showed how interested he was in all those juicy-looking steaks out there. I stopped the truck to begin scattering the hay and left Shep inside as I didn't want him spooking the elk away. His window was open, but he was obedient enough that he would never jump through it unless he was ordered to do so. The elk were still standing a few yards away, keeping an anxious eye on their most ancient enemy. By the time I'd climbed up onto the load to undo the ropes that held the hay, the elk were growing impatient with my progress. They began stomping their feet, snorting, and giving off a few wheezy whistles—but they were not quite bold enough to come right up to the truck, hay or no hay. This was an interesting situation to watch, to see how far things might be teased along,

I threw down the first hay so that it landed right under Shep's open window. After that I sat down to see what would happen. For a minute or two nobody made a move, then a big old cow sidled over and grabbed a mouthful of hay that was only about eight feet from Shep's nose. I couldn't see him from where I was sitting, but all of a sudden he let out one of his famous roars, a growl so ferocious it would have sent any sensible animal right up to the top of the mountain. Instead, the cow stood her ground, sticking her head almost inside the truck and letting out a snort that must have blown snot all over the inside of the cab. By that time Shep was raising holy hell in there, but that cow just kept snorting, shaking her head, and stamping her feet at him. If it wasn't affecting Shep it sure as hell was getting to me, because I began to wonder how safe the truck door was going to be.

This cow must have been the head honcho, because when the whole scene began, the rest of the elk had run off a ways to form a semi-circle and watch the show, just as I was doing. After a few moments of this stand-off, however, about ten elk warily returned to the truck and arranged themselves so that they had the entire front-end surrounded, almost shoulder to shoulder. And as soon as they were in formation they started stamping and snorting too, so there was quite a noisy commotion going on down there. It took only another minute or so until most of the elk began rearing up and making striking motions towards the cab. By now Shep was dancing around so furiously that he had the whole truck rocking. From the sound of his roars I knew he was well over onto the driver's side of the cab— probably as far away from that open window as he could get.

I sympathized with him. If I'd stood only 30 inches at the shoulder I would have been doing exactly the same thing. A few minutes passed before I decided to put an end to the ruckus, by which point there seemed every possibility the elk would begin demolishing the doors. I stood up on the top of the load of hay and began hollering and waving my arms at the elk, only to discover that the situation had perhaps been allowed to go too far, because the only reaction from the elk was to lay back their ears and begin flailing their front feet towards me as well.

I'd obviously made a few miscalculations about elk, and though I didn't consider myself to be in any particular danger, it was still unsettling enough that I wanted out of the deadlock as soon as possible. Shep had stopped barking and I couldn't see what he was up to. It crossed my mind to order him out of the truck so he could put the run on these elk, but I decided against it for two reasons. First, I did not want the elk to become overly afraid of me or of the truck. Second, I was becoming skeptical whether the herd of elk would actually turn and run from a lone dog. The next best thing I could think of was to simply throw some hay as far away from the truck as I could, and as soon as the elk went after it I would slide down into the cab, drive off a ways, and start over again.

As usual, things did not go according to plan. Some of the elk did shift over and begin to feed on the new hay, but they drew newcomers out of the bush and in no time at all there were something like 30 elk around the truck—all of them acting just as bold as the first ones. As a matter of fact, some of them marched right up to the truck and began feeding off the sides of it.

It was about then that I decided my best course of action was to slide down onto the roof of the cab, proceed onto the hood, and make a dash for the door. But when some of those older cows saw what I was up to, they charged right over and chased me back up on top of that load of hay again. They even topped it off by giving a demonstration of how, if they really wanted to, they might be able to reach up high enough to knock me off the load. I was left in no doubt that they could easily have knocked me off the top of the cab.

I had to do something quickly, because the idea of sitting there while they ate the hay out from under me did not have much appeal. I decided to take off my mackinaw and shake it at them, and this did work to a small degree initially. Most of them moved off a few yards. Within no time at all, however, a few simply trotted around the truck to resume feeding on the other side of me. The effect was so minimal it was easy to see that within a few more minutes the coat trick would be of no use whatsoever.

The best manoeuvre now seemed to be to reverse this silly situation, bail right off the load, and make a direct run straight at them, perhaps shaking the coat at the same time. After all, everybody knows that no wild animal will stand up to that type of human assault.

I'd just settled on this course of action when I had a moment's pause. As I was kneeling down to slide off the back end of the load, several of those old cows stopped eating and stood there staring at me with looks of curiosity on their faces, but no real sign of fear. It got me to wondering whether the stories we hear as kids—about animals having telepathic powers—might have a bit of truth to them. But I quickly remembered that I wasn't much of a kid anymore, reminding myself that those stories were all just bullshit. It was now or never.

Before making the final slide I began shaking the coat and hollering, the idea being that it might be wise to get the elk at least a bit spooked up before I hit the ground. As it turned out, those stupid old bitches never even moved. Well, so what? Who in hell is afraid of a few cow elk? I'd never heard of anybody getting eaten by one. All the same, a sort of quiver from my heart muscles reminded me that there was probably still a lot I didn't know about elk. So much for that plan.

By now I'd been treed, or more accurately "hayed," by these animals for about half an hour and the entire situation was becoming as frustrating as hell. I knew there had to be a simple and safe way out of the dilemma, but nothing would come to mind. So I sat down and decided to think the whole thing through to a rational conclusion. One thing about it all, though: watching the elk munch away on the hay wasn't a bad way of passing the time—it was almost like being at a tea party with a lot of lady elks. It was easy to see that the elk were enjoying this visit every bit as much as, and perhaps more than, I was. They calmed right down to some serious eating, belching, and farting and were paying almost no attention to me at all. Not only that, but there was no more noise or movement from inside the truck, and the elk were not even looking in anymore, so I suspected that my loyal partner was now bedded down on the floor.

While all of this was just as interesting as hell, I knew I could not stay there all day, and my next brainwave came when I remembered one of our old cowboy tricks. This was a ploy we used to make sulky yearling cattle move on those occasions when they refuse to do so. With a cattle herd we spot out the laziest actor, toss a rope onto it, drag it back behind the herd a ways, tie a tin can onto either its tail or neck, and then turn it loose. I tell you, that tin-canned cow will take off up the trail like a singed cat, looking for help from its buddies. At the sight and sound of its return to the herd, its ex-friends want nothing to do with it and it's a great and amusing way to get a fast four miles out of the whole bunch. In my cowboying days, this method was usually used only when there was no boss with us, because there were too many campfire stories about what had happened to spooked herds over the years. The old Texas drovers had one word for this experience: stampede.

Unfortunately, I didn't have a tin can with me, but I did have a long piece of plastic rope that had been used to tie down the hay. I cut off a twelve-foot length and tied a loose eye in one end, which gave me a poor man's lariat. This type of rope is not ideal for throwing, but it does have enough weight to fly a short way and that seemed to be all I needed. The eye, or honda, consisted of one half-hitch knot that would come undone easily—I had no intention of trying to wrestle one of these old girls to the ground. I planned to tie my coat to the opposite end, so that when I roped an elk the flying mackinaw would have the effect of guaranteeing that this particular elk herd would be sponging its next hay meal down in Jackson Hole, Wyoming.

As I was putting my rigging together I knew everything was going to work according to plan, as how could it *not* work? Before I went ahead, another brainwave told me that there was no need to sacrifice the coat since wild elk are not used to having anything at all put on them. So the rope alone would do the trick. Aside from the fact that the coat was almost new and had cost me $30 in Williams Lake, if the knot didn't give soon enough, or didn't give at all, it was going to be rather embarrassing to explain to my bosses and neighbours just how I'd lost it. There and then I decided not to tell anybody about this situation because I'd just remembered that Ray or Dave had asked me to keep human contact with these animals to a minimum.

The angle from the top of the load was such that I ended up missing on my first three attempts to lasso an elk. When the rope had touched those old girls, though, it was obvious they didn't like the feel of it any more than I thought they would. Not only that, but once again they astounded me with how quickly they learned and adapted. After the third throw, every elk in that herd had figured out how to duck a loop; no wild horses I ever saw learned as fast as those elk did. And were those elk ever swift with the dodge! Three strikes with the rope and now here they were, simply running up to the truck with their heads down low, grabbing a mouthful of hay, then jumping back about 50 feet to where they could stand and nonchalantly munch it down. The whole time they were also watching every move I made with the most mischievous looks any animal is capable of portraying. They have amazingly expressive faces.

It took me no time at all to figure out how to outmanoeuvre them, and that was to set the rope as a snare. Now, finally, it was my turn to grin, because when I jerked the rope up around an old cow's neck she jumped high enough to have landed on top of that load with me. Luckily, though, she took off through the herd, bucking and twisting harder than any rodeo bronc, and she created such a panic among the others that within three seconds there was not an elk in sight.

It took me about the same span of time to leap down off my unintended perch, and when my feet hit the ground the situation was mine to control again. There was no evidence that my bouncy friends were interested in coming out of the bush while I was still there. Checking in on my partner in the truck, I discovered that he'd curled up on the floor under the steering wheel, and when I invited him to come out and stretch his legs he would not even look at me. From that day on, whenever Shep was with me in the truck and we got close to elk, no matter where we were, he would just curl up on the seat or floor and refuse to raise his head to so much as look at them. He wouldn't even bark or growl at them. That day was quite an experience and it's replayed in my memory many times since. It's the kind of experience a person would willingly go through again, but for me, alas, that's never happened.

Returning Home

In many ways that winter turned out to be much too short. Just as I was beginning to feel I had a firm grip on things, the wind changed and announced that it was Rocky Mountain springtime and the feeding program was over. The smell of that spring also told me that it was time to return to my own world in the Chilcotin, that a pleasant interlude was over.

It had lasted long enough to teach me that elk are as fascinating as I'd previously been told, and the experience whetted my appetite enough to launch me into years of scheming thoughts on how to attract those beautiful animals back to their former range in the Chilcotin. I've always believed in the theory that if a person thinks, prays, and schemes long enough, positive things will almost always come about. So even though there hasn't been a noticeable increase in the Chilcotin elk population, I do believe that one way or another there will be another Chilcotin elk herd—hopefully a big one.

My education was not completely over, however, because for my last day in East Kootenay, Ray Demarchi and Dave Phelps invited me to tag along, observe, and help with an actual CRMP work bee—one that was not taking place in an office. I learned that I was to participate in one of the early, legal, range-burning programs. When we arrived at the site, several ranchers, hunters, and outfitters joined us, along with an entire Forest Service fire suppression crew that was training in the area. The Forest Service arrived with a truckload of "drip torches," a mechanical device for starting fires when firefighters are "back-firing" a forest fire. But this time their use was reversed. What we did was burn off a section of grassland that had been so overused that it was producing mostly weeds and sagebrush. The long-term hope was that the grassland would return to something approximating what it had been, and most of the evidence shows it usually does.

The weather was perfect that day, and we got what was considered a good burn. What I remember most is the image of those Forest Rangers lighting up the countryside. Before then, every Forest Ranger I'd ever met had been in the greatest sweat to put out even the tiniest spark, but these fellows looked to be the most enthusiastic fire bugs that the devil could ever hope for, and to me, that was an education in itself.

Since then there have been many legal range burnings in B.C., most of them beneficial to domestic and wild grazers. At the same time, we should not pat ourselves on the back too much for our management efforts, because what some people were calling a new theory had actually been used deliberately by humans as far back as prehistoric times. All we were doing was relearning how to live with nature rather than continuously trying to reinvent it.

The idea of relearning is not always easy to get across to some people because modern civilization has created what we recognize today as a new breed of technocrat, people who are out to prove—at everything else's expense—that they are an improvement over God. Oh sure they are! Do you believe that chemical fertilizers, herbicides, and pesticides are better than thousands of years of tried and proven burning techniques?

Not long after my return to the Chilcotin, the CRMP system was tried here, too, but it did not last long. We didn't have enough local backing that was not pro-industry. So now industry and the B.C. Forest Service seem to have regained control of the entire resource pie, and they allocate it pretty much at their discretion. To do this, they maintain what are called public-input systems, but the rules and even the buzz-phrases, such as CRMP, have changed. Now there are new buzzwords, such as LRMPs, and the rules at the table have reverted to "the District Forest Manager reserves the right to make final decisions."

Anybody who goes to the resource-use tables these days is there in only an *advisory* capacity. When you think of resource allocation, do the figures of 12 percent and 88 percent sound

Lawson Sugden was the first wildlife biologist in the Cariboo–Chilcotin during the early 1950s. I never met him at that time, but he's come back since to see and hear how it all turned out, and we have had interesting conversations on the subject. He seems to wince a bit when I expound my opinions on the present vintage of wildlife biologists, which always seem to include a question on the strength of their spines, especially when dealing with smokestack technocrats like the B.C. Forest Service or Ministry of Agriculture. Here I am with Lawson and Carolyn Sugden, and my four-legged friend Zoo, at Gaspard Lake in 1999.

like sharing to you? When I grew up, the system taught by my parents was that sharing meant something a lot closer to half-and-half.

Passing the Torch

Well, partner, we have just passed into a new century and a new millennium, so it's also time to pass the torch on to you. It comes with fair warning about the way things are, though, because that torch may not turn out to be a very nice gift. For starters, the politicians, bureaucrats, and industry people have just taken us back into something like the Dark Ages with their newest buzz-formula for resources. The whole shebang is now being administered through what's called Inter-Agency Cooperation, which is about where we were around the year 1900. To compound that problem, there are few, if any, new resource managers around today who can measure up to the calibre of Harold Mitchell, Ray Demarchi, Daryl Hebert, Dave Phelps, and a few others.

At the last public-input meeting I attended, the new managers of our wildlife and environment had about as much backbone as a jellyfish when discussing issues with industry and the Ministry of Forests. From what I can see, this new breed will never consider putting their jobs on the line to back up their convictions, even if they have any.

If we're not careful we'll wake up to find most of our Crown resources licensed out in tree farms, game farms, fish farms, closed cattle ranges, and huge commercial tourist attractions. And that means you and I will have to pay somebody every time we step out of our house or our vehicle. All I can say is that to this old warrior, Inter-Agency Cooperation is enough to make a person puke.

Cheers from Chilicootin.

Born for the Wild Country
Big Feet and a Mouth to Match
Chilco Choate

ISBN 1-895811-59-7
5½ x 8½ • 192 pages
Softcover • $17.95

Ted "Chilco" Choate vividly remembers the "powerful per-
sonalities" that helped prepare him for life in the back country.
Skunks, raccoons, schoolteachers, and game wardens influenced
Chilco's philosophy, which he shares with wit, wisdom, and
respect for the individuality in all of us.

On Becoming Retired, Year 2000

I've ridden all over this country, and I'll say that man will never find trails more peaceful and mellow than the ones that are blazed to the meadow on this beautiful Chilcotin Plateau. I tried to get out of this country, but poverty forced me to stay, until I became an old-timer, then no logger, rancher, or ranger, could ever chase me away. No longer a slave of ambition, I laugh at the rest as they fall on their ass, as I soak into my wonderful condition, surrounded by mountains and valleys of grass.

Chilco Choate was born into the Great Depression, and after a Huck Finn youth, left home at sixteen, bound for the Chilcotin country. He tried cowboying but soon became a big-game guide and outfitter. A half century later he remains on the shoreline of Gaspard Lake with a lifetime of yarns and experience to help guide his pen.